Learn OpenGL ES

For Mobile Game and Graphics Development

Prateek Mehta

Apress·

Learn OpenGL ES

ISBN-13 (pbk): 978-1-4302-5053-1

ISBN-13 (electronic): 978-1-4302-5054-8

President and Publisher: Paul Manning
Lead Editor: Steve Anglin
Developmental Editor: Tom Welsh
Technical Reviewer: Shane Kirk
Editorial Board: Steve Anglin, Mark Beckner, Ewan Buckingham, Gary Cornell, Louise Corrigan, Morgan Ertel, Jonathan Gennick, Jonathan Hassell, Robert Hutchinson, Michelle Lowman, James Markham, Matthew Moodie, Jeff Olson, Jeffrey Pepper, Douglas Pundick, Ben Renow-Clarke, Dominic Shakeshaft, Gwenan Spearing, Matt Wade, Tom Welsh
Coordinating Editor: Jill Balzano
Copy Editor: Lori Cavanaugh
Compositor: SPi Global
Indexer: SPi Global
Artist: SPi Global
Cover Designer: Anna Ishchenko

Distributed to the book trade worldwide by Springer Science+Business Media New York, 233 Spring Street, 6th Floor, New York, NY 10013. Phone 1-800-SPRINGER, fax (201) 348-4505, e-mail orders-ny@springer-sbm.com, or visit www.springeronline.com. Apress Media, LLC is a California LLC and the sole member (owner) is Springer Science + Business Media Finance Inc (SSBM Finance Inc). SSBM Finance Inc is a Delaware corporation.

For information on translations, please e-mail rights@apress.com, or visit www.apress.com.

Apress and friends of ED books may be purchased in bulk for academic, corporate, or promotional use. eBook versions and licenses are also available for most titles. For more information, reference our Special Bulk Sales–eBook Licensing web page at www.apress.com/bulk-sales.

Any source code or other supplementary materials referenced by the author in this text is available to readers at www.apress.com. For detailed information about how to locate your book's source code, go to www.apress.com/source-code/.

Dedicated to my parents and my brother for their everlasting support and encouragement.
And to the Stack Overflow community, for making computer programming less troublesome.

Contents at a Glance

Contents

About the Author

Prateek Mehta (pixdip.com/admin/about.html) is pursuing his
B.Tech. degree in Information Technology Engineering at the
Indraprastha University. He is a Web and OpenGL ES application
developer, and is currently building up a graphic dev-tool based on
Apache Flex. He is awaiting collaborators for his Perl parser for Blender
geometry definition files (bitbucket.org/prateekmehta). This parser has
been made use of in this book.

Prateek lives in South West Delhi and, when not doing technical things,
works as a freelance lyricist. He spends his spare time playing
Counter-Strike, "de_dust2", and "de_inferno" are his favorite maps,
where he is busy sniping with his AWP.

On Stack Overflow he has a keen interest in answering questions
tagged under "css" and "opengl-es-2.0".

About the Technical Reviewer

Shane Kirk earned his B.S. in Computer Science from the University of Kentucky in 2000. He's currently a software engineer for IDEXX Laboratories in Westbrook, Maine, where he spends his days working with enterprise Java. He's also a very enthusiastic Android developer with a strong interest in building mobile solutions for working musicians. When Shane isn't coding, you can usually find him holed up in his home studio working on the next album from his band The Wee Lollies (www.theweelollies.com).

Acknowledgments

My sincere thanks go to:

Steve Anglin, for giving me this wonderful opportunity to write for Apress. Steve, I am grateful for the time you spent guiding me away from my paranoia about publishing companies. Now, I'm so much away from it, that I can't help myself from writing another book, very soon!

My editors, **Tom Welsh** and **Jill Balzano**. I really appreciate their patience for putting up with a first-time author. Jill, "freeze frame" high five for sorting out all the problems during the writing of this book. Tom, thanks for getting me baptized in the river of revision - gennick.com/sm.html.

Lori Cavanaugh, my copy editor, for putting the finishing touches on the manuscripts, and also my tech reviewer **Shane Kirk** for his helpful insights. Shane, you were really spot on with those excellent suggestions, and I've no idea how you balance the beats and bytes.

My mentors, **Dr. Atul Kumar** and **Dr. Alok K. Kushwaha**, for their crucial support and encouragement.

My friends, **Anupam** and **Sheetanshu**, for providing useful support for Android devices, and also my pro-gamer comrade, **Tejas**, for exhibiting his amazing photography skills.

Preface

This book takes Android app developers through the development of interactive OpenGL ES 2.0 applications; they will also absorb the fundamental concepts of rendering 3D graphics on Android using OpenGL ES 2.0.

OpenGL ES 2.0 is derived from the extensive OpenGL 2.0 API, which is a popular API for rendering 3D graphics on desktops. In fact ES 2.0 is a form of this API, optimized for use on low power display devices such as mobiles and tablets.

OpenGL ES 2.0 is a programmable graphic rendering API, so understanding it is similar to understanding WebGL for browsers, Direct3D or OpenGL for desktops, or Stage3D on Flash. This version offers greater flexibility than OpenGL ES 1.x in rendering 3D graphics, as it implements the long-awaited *GLSL* shading language.

OpenGL ES 2.0 on Android enables programmers to create interactive as well as non-interactive graphics applications. However, compared to non-interactive ES 2.0 applications like *Live Wallpapers*, interactive ES 2.0 applications are more challenging to create because they demand greater focus on the part of the developer.

Applications are said to be interactive when user inputs dictate changes in their appearance. With Android SDK, interactive ES 2.0 applications can be conveniently developed because no external libraries are required to use the OpenGL ES 2.0 API. Moreover, accessing other features of Android handhelds such as motion/position sensors, audio, and so on, along with the OpenGL ES 2.0 API does not require much effort. The Android SDK suffices to create most modern interactive ES 2.0 applications, such as image-editing software, games, and a lot more.

My focus will be to create a simple shooting game, using touch and motion/position sensors, that will help you to understand important concepts like *Buffers*, *GLSL*, *State Management*, and *3D-Transformation* for developing interactive ES 2.0 applications on Android. So, let's *Learn OpenGL ES* for mobile game and graphics development.

Chapter 1

Benefits of the New API

In this chapter I introduce you to OpenGL ES 2.0, and account for its increasing popularity compared to older graphic rendering APIs for embedded devices. I describe OpenGL ES 2.0's support from computer-graphics communities and leading embedded and mobile device vendors, which helps to ensure its increasing popularity. Finally, I show how easy it is to get started with ES 2.0 on Android devices, when we take our first step towards game development, by creating a blank OpenGL surface view.

This chapter assumes you have some experience of setting up Android Software Development Kit (SDK) for Eclipse and installing SDK Platform for various API levels from SDK Manager.

Modern Graphic-rendering API

OpenGL ES (Open Graphics Library for Embedded Systems) is an API (Application Programming Interface) for rendering 3D graphics on embedded devices, such as mobiles, tablets, and gaming consoles.

The OpenGL ES 1.0 and ES 1.1 APIs (referred to jointly as OpenGL ES 1.x) were released by the non-profit *Khronos Group* as a fixed-function graphic-rendering API. OpenGL ES 1.x API does not provide graphics application developers full access to underlying hardware, because most rendering functions in this API are hard-coded, leading to popular names—"fixed-function graphic rendering API" or "fixed-function pipeline."

Unlike OpenGL ES 1.x API, OpenGL ES 2.0 API was released as a programmable graphic-rendering API (programmable pipeline), giving developers full access to the underlying hardware through *shaders* (discussed in Chapter 3).

Graphics rendered through a fixed-function pipeline involve device-provided algorithms for most rendering effects. These algorithms (and the rendering functions based on them) cannot be modified. They are fixed because they were made for special purpose graphics cards, for a specific data-flow. Because of the fixed functionality of OpenGL ES 1.x API, graphics hardware could be optimized for faster rendering.

In contrast, a programmable graphic-rendering API is a more flexible API and requires a general purpose graphics card, enabling graphic developers to unleash the huge potential of modern GPUs. Technically, the programmable pipeline is slower than the fixed function pipeline; however, graphics rendered using the programmable pipeline can be greatly enhanced because of flexibility offered by new general purpose graphics cards. OpenGL ES 2.0 combines *GLSL (OpenGL Shading Language)* with a modified subset of OpenGL ES 1.1 that has removed any fixed functionality. Chapter 3 discusses OpenGL Shading Language.

> **Note**   *GLSL* is the OpenGL Shading Language for programming vertex and fragment shaders. Shaders are programs in programmable pipelines that help users work on two separate aspects of object rendering: vertex marking and color filling.

With OpenGL ES 2.0, enhancements in various effects, such as lighting/shading effects (as shown in Figure 1-1—a basic shading example), no longer have any restrictions, compared to ES 1.x. What is required is transformation of creative ideas for any such effects into algorithms, then into custom functions executed on the graphics card, which would be impossible in ES 1.x.

Figure 1-1. ADS (Ambient Diffuse Specular) shading in OpenGL ES 2.0

OpenGL ES 2.0 is derived from the larger OpenGL 2.0 API, the programmable pipeline for rendering 3D graphics on desktops. ES 2.0 is a suitable subset of OpenGL, optimized for resource constrained display devices, such as mobiles, tablets, and gaming consoles. ES 2.0 contains only the most useful methods from OpenGL 2.0 API, with redundant techniques removed. This allows OpenGL ES 2.0 on handheld devices to deliver rich game content like its parent API.

Devices Love It

As of October 1, 2012, more than 90% of all Android devices were running version 2.0 of OpenGL ES. Devices running version 2.0 are also capable of emulating version 1.1. However, an activity in Android cannot use both versions together, stemming from the fact that OpenGL ES 2.0 API is not backwards compatible with ES 1.x. Note that, although an *activity* cannot use both versions together, an *application* can still use them together. (Information about OpenGL ES version distribution across Android devices is available at `http://developer.android.com/about/dashboards/index.html`, and Figure 1–2 shows a chart representing that distribution.)

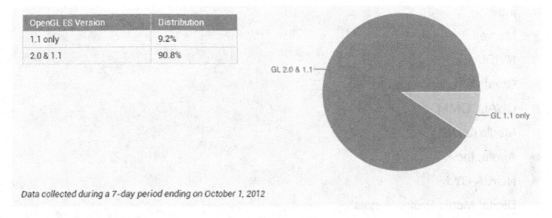

OpenGL ES Version	Distribution
1.1 only	9.2%
2.0 & 1.1	90.8%

Data collected during a 7-day period ending on October 1, 2012

Figure 1-2. *OpenGL ES version distribution*

> **Note**   To demonstrate the use of both ES 1.x and ES 2.0 APIs in an application, the *GLES ACTIVITY* application is provided in the source code for this chapter. This application contains activities `Main` and `Second`. The `Main` activity uses ES 1.x, whereas the `Second` activity uses ES 2.0. To load this application into your Eclipse workspace, under "File Menu," select "Import," and then import the archive file `glesactivity.zip` from the `Chapter1` folder.

OpenGL ES 2.0 constitutes such a huge share of distribution (Figure 1-2), because of widespread support from leading CPU and GPU manufacturing industries. (A complete list of companies with their conformant ES 1.x/2.0 products can be found at `http://www.khronos.org/conformance/adopters/conformant-products#opengles`.) The following vendors have actively participated in consolidating support for OpenGL ES 2.0 on Android since 2010:

(Leading GPU manufacturers)

- NVIDIA
- AMD
- Imagination Technologies

(Leading CPU manufacturers)

- ARM
- Texas Instruments
- STMicroelectronics

Implementer companies make use of the *Khronos developed technologies* at no cost in license fees. However, they do not claim that a product is "compliant," unless the technologies enter and pass conformance testing. The following are the implementers of OpenGL ES 2.0 for various embedded devices:

- Intel
- Marvell
- NVIDIA
- Creative Technology Ltd.
- QUALCOMM
- MediaTek Inc.
- Apple, Inc.
- NOKIA OYJ
- Digital Media Professionals
- Panasonic

> **Note**   Although most embedded platforms are up and running with OpenGL ES 2.0, the Khronos Group announced on August 6th, 2012, the release of the OpenGL ES 3.0 specification, bringing significant functionality and portability enhancements to OpenGL ES API. OpenGL ES 3.0 is backwards compatible with OpenGL ES 2.0, enabling applications to incrementally add new visual features to applications. The full specification and reference materials are available for immediate download at `http://www.khronos.org/registry/gles/`.

Easy App Development: Let's Create an OpenGL Surface View

ES 2.0 applications can be easily developed for Android devices using the Android SDK. The best part about creating such applications using this SDK is that there is no need for any external library (something that can be quite burdensome for new ES 2.0 application developers on iPhone).

There is another way to create Android ES 2.0 applications—using the Android *Native Development Kit* (*NDK*). In some cases, NDK can make ES 2.0 applications faster than those made using SDK. NDK lets users code in native languages, such as C and C++. This makes it possible to use popular libraries written using C/C++, but only at the cost of increased complexity. Beginner ES 2.0 application developers may find this difficult to deal with, which can ultimately make NDK counter-productive. NDK is typically a tool for advanced Android developers, but be assured the performance gap between most ES 2.0 applications created using SDK and NDK is becoming negligible.

> **Note**   Do not use NDK simply because you like coding your applications in C/C++; use it only for cases in which performance is critical to your application. Also, remember that Dalvik VM is becoming faster, reducing the performance gap between SDK and NDK.

Determining OpenGL ES Version

To demonstrate the ease of developing ES 2.0 applications for Android devices, a quick example is given here for creating an OpenGL surface view. This view is different from the XML view (UI layout) you have generally created for most Android applications. (Chapter 3 contains a detailed account of OpenGL surface view.)

Before I discuss this example, you need to determine the version of OpenGL ES on your Android device. To do so, let's create a blank `Activity`:

1. In the Eclipse toolbar, click the icon to open wizard to create a new Android project.

2. Uncheck the "Create custom launcher icon" option, and click "Next," as shown in Figure 1-3.

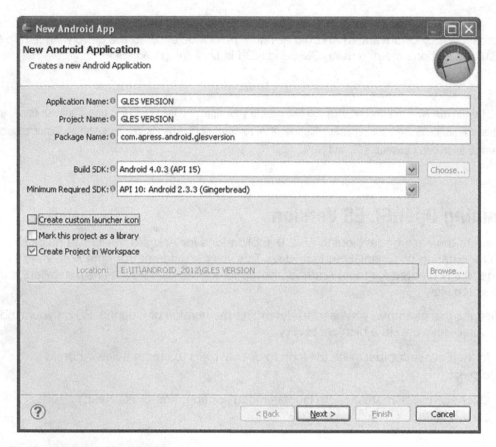

Figure 1-3. Creating a new Android application

Note   You might be accustomed to an older version of the SDK. The older version lacked some tools present in the newer version. Make sure you have these tools installed using your SDK Manager. If you prefer working offline, always allow time to update the SDK.

3. For "Create Activity," select BlankActivity and click "Next." Select MasterDetailFlow (Figure 1-4) only if you are experienced in developing applications for tablets. This book only addresses BlankActivity, because we are not developing for tablets.

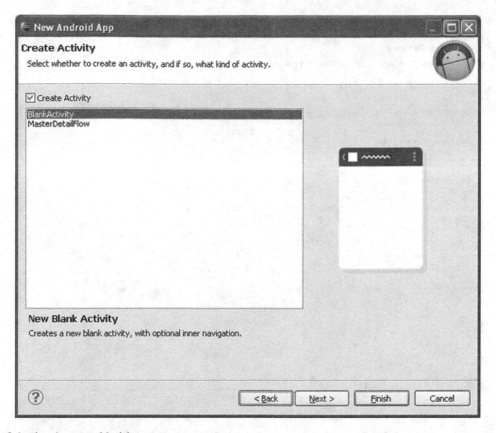

Figure 1-4. Selecting the type of Activity

4. Set the "Activity Name" and "Layout Name" as "Main" and "main,"
    respectively (Figure 1-5). In cases in which the Android application has only
    one activity, most coders name the Java file Main.java.

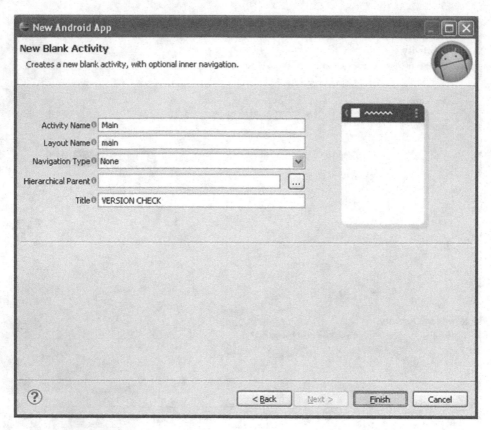

Figure 1-5. Creating a new blank Activity

5. Click "Finish" if you have already installed the "Android Support Library."
    If you haven't installed it, then click "Install/Update," wait until it is installed,
    and then click "Finish" (please note that you might not get the option to
    install "Android Support Library" if using an older version of the ADT plugin).

After the blank Activity (Main.java) is created, SDK will show warnings for unused imports, as shown in Figure 1-6. To remove these warnings:

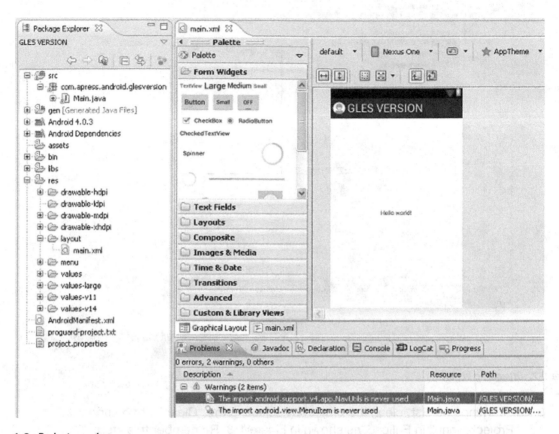

Figure 1-6. Project warnings

1. In the *Problems* view, click the small plus-sign (+) button near "Warnings" and the list of warnings will be displayed.

2. Double click any warning. SDK will move the edit cursor to the line containing the warning.

3. Now, press *Ctrl* and *1* on the keyboard. SDK will then suggest ways to remove the warning(s).

4. Select the "Organize imports" (Figure 1-7) option, and the warnings will be removed.

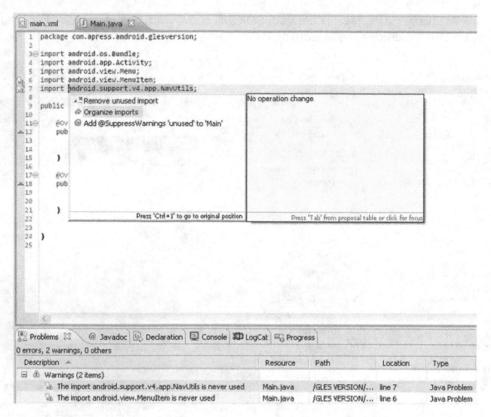

Figure 1-7. Organizing imports

5. If warnings persist, clean the project by selecting the "Clean" option under "Project Menu" in Eclipse, as shown in Figure 1-8. Remember this step, because Eclipse might not update the project binaries after modification(s). Cleaning will update/refresh them.

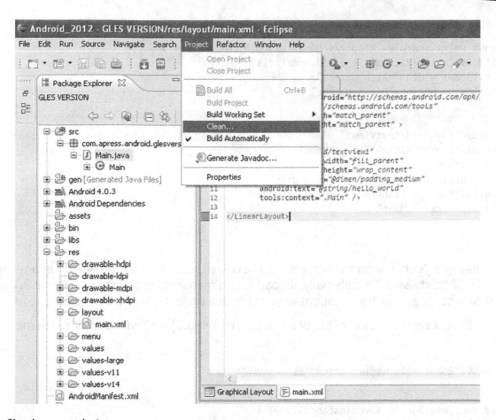

Figure 1-8. Cleaning our project

> **Note**   Although it is not necessary to remove all the warnings from your application (because the application can still work with these warnings), get into the habit of clearing them, especially in cases in which unused imports or other redundant code can cause your application to be larger than necessary.
>
> The few lines that cause warnings may look insignificant now; however, later in the book, we will be dealing with examples in which those lines might add up to bloat the performance of your application. The Android *lint* tool always highlights such warnings and, in some cases, can optimize the binaries by itself. This does not happen always, however, so remember to clear those warnings.

After warnings have been removed, replace the entire (XML) UI layout in your project's res/layout/ main.xml with the contents of Listing 1-1. Notice the main difference between Listing 1-1 and the default UI layout (of the blank Activity template) is the root tag RelativeLayout.

Listing 1-1. GLES VERSION/res/layout/main.xml

```xml
<LinearLayout xmlns:android="http://schemas.android.com/apk/res/android"
    xmlns:tools="http://schemas.android.com/tools"
    android:layout_width="match_parent"
    android:layout_height="match_parent" >

    <TextView
        android:id="@+id/textview1"
        android:layout_width="fill_parent"
        android:layout_height="wrap_content"
        android:padding="@dimen/padding_medium"
        android:text="@string/hello_world"
        tools:context=".Main" />

</LinearLayout>
```

Listing 1-1 places a `TextView` on the screen. This `TextView` is as wide as the screen in any orientation and has an `id` of "textview1." Additionally, its padding-dimensions and text are defined in the `dimens.xml` and `strings.xml` files, respectively, inside this project's *res/values* folder.

Now, replace the `onCreate` method of the blank `Activity` (`Main.java`) with the `onCreate` method from Listing 1-2.

Listing 1-2. GLES VERSION/src/com/apress/android/glesversion/Main.java

```java
@Override
public void onCreate(Bundle savedInstanceState) {
  super.onCreate(savedInstanceState);
  setContentView(R.layout.main);

  final ActivityManager activityManager = (ActivityManager) getSystemService(Context.ACTIVITY_SERVICE);
  final ConfigurationInfo configurationInfo = activityManager.getDeviceConfigurationInfo();
  final boolean supportsEs2 = configurationInfo.reqGlEsVersion >= 0x20000;

  TextView tv = (TextView) findViewById(R.id.textview1);
  if (supportsEs2) {
    tv.setText("es2 is supported");
  } else {
    tv.setText("es2 is not supported");
  }
}
```

In the `onCreate` method (Listing 1-2), we obtain the device configuration attributes and use them to detect the version of OpenGL ES running on the device. Next, we find the `TextView` in the UI layout of our application by its `id` ("textview1") and use it to display the result using its `setText` method.

Now the application is ready for use. However, before running this application on a real device, we will test it on the Android Emulator. If you haven't created a virtual device yet, start the AVD Manager and complete the following steps:

1. Click "New" to open the window to create a new virtual device.

2. Name this virtual device "IceCreamSandwich". We are targeting (at least) the Ice Cream Sandwich emulator, so we will name it IceCreamSandwich. You may also modify this name to indicate the resolution of virtual device.

3. Under target, select API level 15, as shown in Figure 1-9.

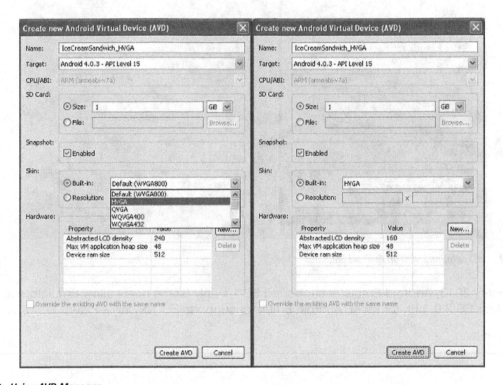

Figure 1-9. Using AVD Manager

4. Enter the size for the SD card.

5. Enable "Snapshot" to avoid going through the Android bootup sequence every time you start the virtual device.

6. To create this virtual device at a specific resolution, select a built-in skin.

7. Click "Create AVD" to create the virtual device.

AVD Manager will take some time to prepare the virtual device. After the device is successfully created, it will be listed in the AVD Manager with a green tick at the beginning. Select the created virtual device and click "Start."

Let the device boot. With *Snapshot* enabled, the device will start from where it left off the next time. When the Home screen is visible in the virtual device (Figure 1-10), return to Eclipse and run the application.

Figure 1-10. IceCreamSandwich on Android Emulator

As of January 2013, Android Emulator supported ES 1.x only (some hosts allow Emulators to access their GPU for ES 2.0, but, for most, Android Emulator supports ES 1.x only—Figure 1-11).

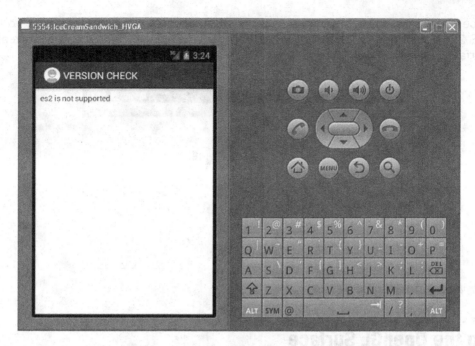

Figure 1-11. Emulator does not support ES 2.0

Now, test this application on a real device. (Here, we use a Motorola Milestone—Figure 1-12—running Gingerbread, Android version 2.3.3). Close the Emulator and connect your Android handheld using USB. Return to Eclipse, and run the application again.

Figure 1-12. Gingerbread on Motorola Milestone

If your device shows "*es2 is not supported*," then try this application on another device you know supports ES 2.0; if your device supports ES 2.0 as shown in Figure 1-13, you can now create an OpenGL surface view. To do so, first you need to create a new Android application.

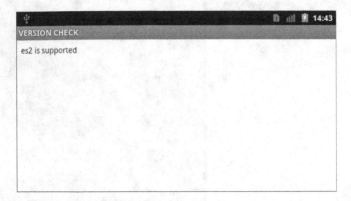

Figure 1-13.   Motorola Milestone supports ES 2.0

Creating the OpenGL Surface

Once you create a new Android application (Figure 1-14), open the Main.java file. Replace the contents of this file with the code given in Listing 1-3. Table 1-1 gives the description of lines in this code.

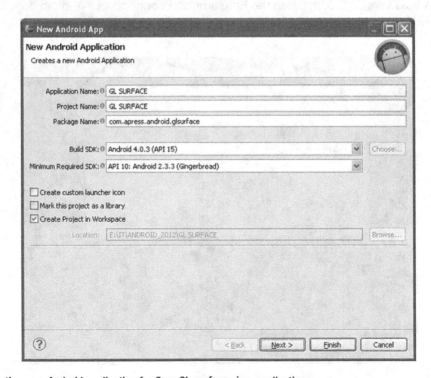

Figure 1-14.   Creating new Android application for OpenGL surface view application

Listing 1-3. GL SURFACE/src/com/apress/android/glsurface/Main.java

```java
public class Main extends Activity {
  private GLSurfaceView _surfaceView;

  @Override
  public void onCreate(Bundle savedInstanceState) {
    super.onCreate(savedInstanceState);
    _surfaceView = new GLSurfaceView(this);
    _surfaceView.setEGLContextClientVersion(2);
    _surfaceView.setRenderer(new GLES20Renderer());
    setContentView(_surfaceView);
  }

}
```

Table 1-1. *onCreate method, lines description*

Line	Description
1.	Calls onCreate method of the super class Activity, which takes Bundle as argument
2.	Requests an OpenGL surface view by calling the view constructor GLSurfaceView, which takes Context as argument
3.	Sets the version of OpenGL ES (in this case, ES 2.0) that will be used by the current context's surface view
4.	Starts a separate renderer thread that will cause the rendering (drawing) to begin
5.	setContentView method sets _surfaceView object as the content view

Because the GLSurfaceView class is not yet imported (Figure 1-15), press *Ctrl* and *1* for quick fixing errors as shown in Figure 1-16. ("Quick fix" is a commonly used problem correction tool in Eclipse.) SDK will import the class, and you will then see only 1 error.

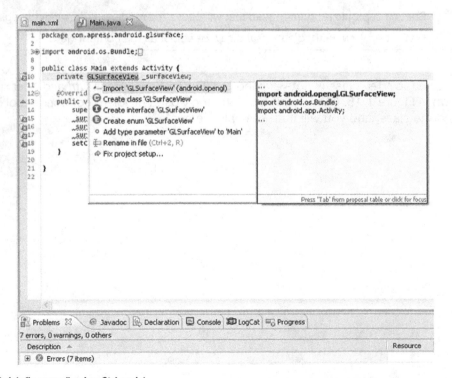

Figure 1-15. *Errors after modifying the template code of class Main*

Figure 1-16. *"Quick fix errors" using Ctrl and 1*

To fix the last error, we have to create the GLES20Renderer class. Amazingly, SDK automates even this step, so you can "quick fix" it. Select the first option (Figure 1-17), to create the class GLES20Renderer, which implements an interface GLSurfaceView.Renderer.

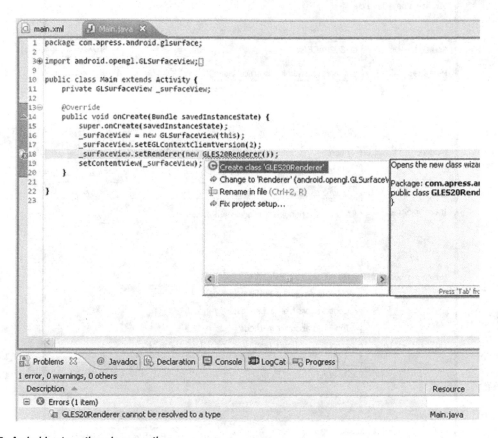

Figure 1-17. Android automating class creation

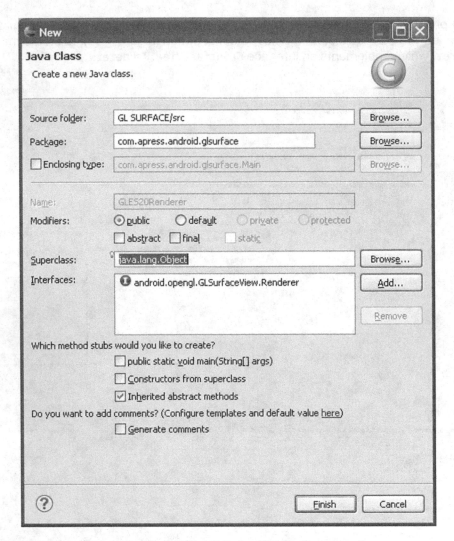

Figure 1-18. GLES20Renderer class implementing interface GLSurfaceView.Renderer

After Android has created our Renderer class (Figure 1-19), you might observe warnings in the *Problems* view, depending on the ADT version you are using. These include:

- The import `android.support.v4.app.NavUtils` is never used.

- The import `android.view.Menu` is never used.

- The import `android.view.MenuItem` is never used.

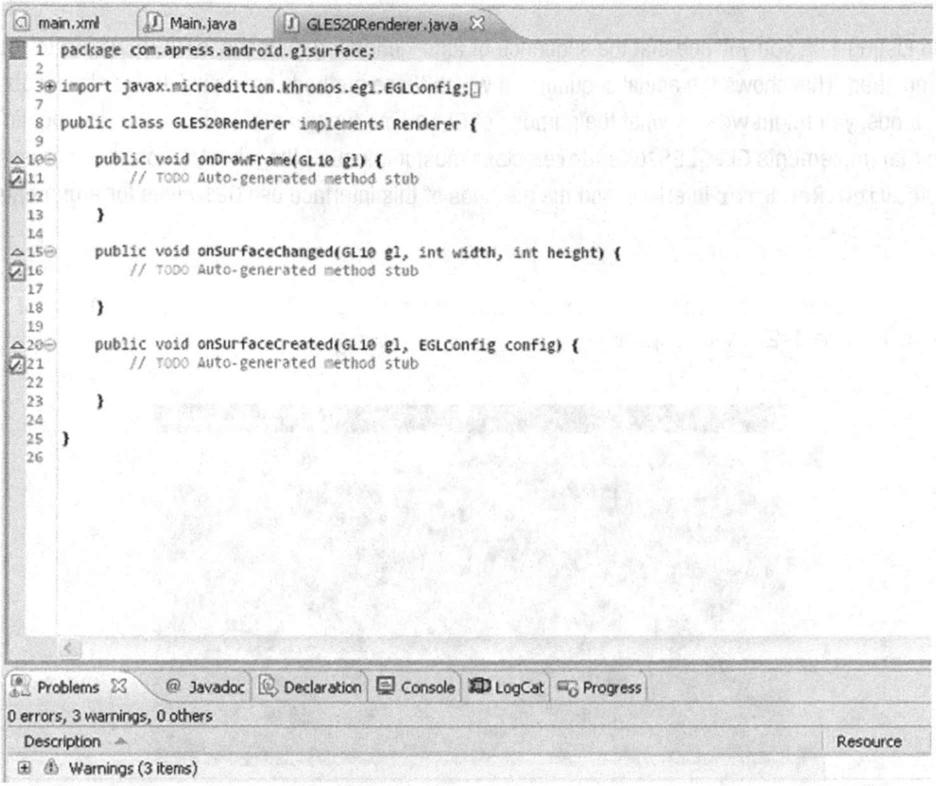

Figure 1-19. Auto-generated methods for GLES20Renderer class

These warnings are indicated for unused imports in Main.java file. Quick fix these warnings if you are on Eclipse. Finally, replace the class GLES20Renderer with the code given in Listing 1-4. You will see an error after replacing the code—"GLES20 cannot be resolved to a variable." This error is caused because the class android.opengl.GLES20 is not imported yet. So, import it.

Listing 1-4. GL SURFACE/src/com/apress/android/glsurface/GLES20Renderer.java

```
public class GLES20Renderer implements Renderer {

  public void onSurfaceCreated(GL10 gl, EGLConfig config) {
    GLES20.glClearColor(0.0f, 0.0f, 1.0f, 1);
  }

  public void onSurfaceChanged(GL10 gl, int width, int height) {
    GLES20.glViewport(0, 0, width, height);
  }

  public void onDrawFrame(GL10 gl) {
    GLES20.glClear(GLES20.GL_COLOR_BUFFER_BIT | GLES20.GL_DEPTH_BUFFER_BIT);
  }

}
```

> **Note**   In Listing 1-4, you will see that the sequence of auto-generated methods for GLES20Renderer class is modified. This shows the actual sequence in which these methods are called. If you closely observe these methods, you might wonder what the purpose of GL10 type for argument gl is. GL10 is a public interface that implements GL. GLES20Renderer class must implement the inherited abstract methods of GLSurfaceView.Renderer interface, and the methods of this interface use GL10 type for arguments.

After removing all errors and warnings, run the application. A blank, blue colored OpenGL surface view, similar to Figure 1-20, will appear.

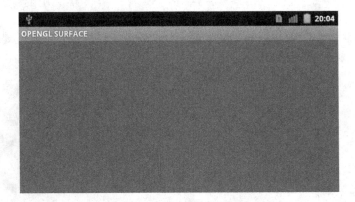

Figure 1-20. Blank OpenGL surface view

Take a closer look at this application's code listings (Listings 1-3 and 1-4). Understanding the structure of such projects and the flow of control will speed up your learning process. Chapters 2 and 3 describe the details of this application, the classes used, the interface Renderer, and the ES 2.0 functions used.

ES 2.0 Is for the Ambitious

As I mentioned earlier, OpenGL ES 2.0 is derived from OpenGL 2.0 API, the programmable pipeline for rendering graphics on desktop hardware. If you are able to understand the concepts behind the programmable pipeline for ES 2.0, you will easily understand OpenGL 2.0 API. It is worth reiterating that OpenGL API is meant only for desktops, not for embedded devices. There are various programming languages you can use to create 3D graphics applications based on OpenGL API, such as Python, C, and C++. Similar to the OpenGL API, there are other programmable graphic rendering APIs (for various platforms), and understanding the OpenGL ES 2.0 API makes understanding the others easy:

- *Direct3D* (the 3D graphics API within Microsoft's DirectX SDK) is also based on programmable pipeline; however, it uses the .NET Framework, not Java, for coding. If you understand the .NET Framework and can code applications in C#, check out *Microsoft XNA* for Windows and Xbox. XNA is a collection of tools that facilitate video game development. XNA Framework is based on the .NET Framework and is the most popular framework for creating 2D/3D games based on the programmable pipeline.

- *Stage3D* and its subset *Starling* are ActionScript 3 3D/2D frameworks used for game development. Stage3D is available on desktop through Flash Player 11 and AIR 3. Stage3D and Starling use low-level GPU APIs running on OpenGL, DirectX on desktop, and OpenGL ES 2.0 on mobiles. If you know how to code in ActionScript 3, you have already mastered one of the prerequisites for Adobe programmable pipeline game development.

- Web Graphics Library (*WebGL*) is a JavaScript API for rendering interactive 2D/3D graphics in web browsers without plug-ins; it can be mixed with HTML. There are many JavaScript libraries for working with WebGL. One is *three.js*, a cross-browser JavaScript library used with HTML5 Canvas. WebGL is based on OpenGL ES 2.0, and, like OpenGL/OpenGL ES, WebGL is designed and maintained by Khronos. Google Maps is one of the most popular WebGL applications. In addition to this, *Chrome Experiments* (Figure 1-21) contains a showcase of various applications powered by WebGL.

Figure 1-21. Chrome Experiments

Chrome Experiments is a showcase for creative web experiments, the vast majority of which are built with the latest open technologies, including HTML5, Canvas, SVG, and WebGL. These were made and submitted by talented artists and programmers from around the world.[1]

The experiments are meant for Chrome browsers, but Mozilla Firefox and Safari are also able to run most of these.

Where Are the Developers?

Most Android devices (more than 90%) have sufficient capabilities to run version 2.0 of OpenGL ES; however, most game developers have not fully exploited such capabilities, because game vendors (i.e., desktop, console, and handheld) develop their own frameworks/engines for creating games and none are completely based on ES 2.0. These frameworks are not designed for multi-paradigm game programming. Instead, they are object-oriented with complete designs for integrating all aspects of the game, mainly:

1. Screen: splash screen, options screen, and game screen

2. Input: keyboard input, touch input, UI input from buttons, and input from motion sensors like Accelerometer and position sensors like Magnetometer, which are common on most Android devices

3. Audio: audio for splash screen and background scores, audio for player/enemy movements and attacks, and audio for options screen and other sounds in the game

It takes time to build and test these game frameworks. The longer it takes to build one, the more variety is offered in terms of types of games. Much literature is available for creating complete game frameworks for Android. The most recent book is *Beginning Android Games, Second Edition* by Mario Zechner and Robert Green (Apress, 2012). *Beginning Android Games* provides a complete idea of how to build an Android game framework; however, all the rendering classes in this book are based on ES 1.0, meaning, once understand ES 2.0, you can translate the fixed functions of ES 1.x into your custom (ES 2.0) functions.

For game developers who have used any open-source or proprietary game development frameworks/engines for handheld devices, based on the fixed-function pipeline, ES 2.0 poses a big problem. However, game developers can take advantage of this situation. They can learn ES 2.0 for developing games, or they can become *game framework developers* for ES 2.0. Because there are few ES 2.0 game developers and even fewer game frameworks, most game developers are also game framework developers.

Here are some popular games on Android based on OpenGL ES 2.0:

■ Death Rally (seen in Figure 1-22) is "an action packed combat racer with cars, guns, and explosive fun. Death Rally has been played more than 60 million times by more than 11 million gamers worldwide!"[2] (More on Remedy Entertainment can be found at `http://remedygames.com`).

---

[1]`http://www.chromeexperiments.com/about/`
[2]`http://remedygames.com`

Figure 1-22. Death Rally by Remedy Entertainment

- ■ "Unlike existing mobile benchmarking applications available for Android enthusiasts, the Electopia OpenGL ES 2.0 benchmark is written by game development experts in a manner representative of advanced, real world mobile games. Electopia provides accurate graphics performance measurements, along with unique features like the ability to isolate GPU performance from other system factors, such as LCD resolution."[3] (More information about Electopia (seen in Figure 1-23) and Tactel can be found at http://electopia1.android.informer.com/).

[3]http://electopia1.android.informer.com/

Figure 1-23. Electopia by Tactel AB

- "Raging Thunder is a gut-churning, tire burning racer, giving you control of the most extreme muscle cars in the world! Race against time, CPU controlled opponents, or up to three other speed addicts in this fast-paced, exhilarating, coin-op style racing game."[4] More about Raging Thunder (seen in Figure 1-24) can be found at https://play.google.com/store/apps/details?id=com.polarbit.ragingthunder.

Figure 1-24. Raging Thunder by polarbit

---

[4]https://play.google.com/store/apps/details?id=com.polarbit.ragingthunder

Summary

This chapter discussed the basic differences between ES 1.x and 2.0 APIs, and how those differences are likely to persist because of the great support for programmable pipeline from leading CPU/GPU hardware manufacturers.

Since learning any new software technology can be difficult, the chapter also features an introductory tour of the vast scope of programmable graphic rendering APIs on various platforms, including modern browsers. It shows you how to create a simple app that makes use of ES 2.0, illustrating how painless it is to use this API on Android using the Android SDK.

In Chapter 2 you can read about some useful techniques for using OpenGL ES with UIs, such as buttons and motion/position sensors, before diving into the ES 2.0 environment for rendering 3D graphics.

Chapter 2

Implementation Prerequisites

This chapter does not jump straight into ES 2.0 fundamentals, because there are some prerequisites, such as knowledge of device inputs, for implementing OpenGL ES on Android devices. Most coders are prone to errors when working with device inputs, which play a crucial role in making ES 2.0 applications interactive, unless they have a sound understanding of the inputs and the associated classes at work behind the scenes.

Before diving into the basic concepts of the programmable pipeline, I shall explain the efficient usage of user interface (UI) on handhelds. You will learn to use buttons to update the rendering on an OpenGL surface and then we will look into using screen and sensors to obtain inputs, which can be used to move and animate game objects.

Selecting a Development Device: Why Upgrade to Gingerbread?

For an interactive graphics application, such as a game, leaving a good impression on users requires fulfilling certain conditions. The most crucial of these is lag time (latency). We often observe delays or lags when interacting with graphics applications, especially during gameplays. This is completely unacceptable, because a few milliseconds can spoil the entire user experience. If developers do not take steps to prevent this, users simply switch to other similar applications that are lag-free.

Although this is not true of earlier Android versions, graphics applications developed on Gingerbread do not suffer from delays or lags. (Reasons for this can be found at http://www.badlogicgames.com/wordpress/?p=1315). Additionally, *Google IO 2011: Memory management for Android Apps*, a conference session held by Google (the video for this session is available on YouTube), explains that pre-Gingerbread garbage collectors are the primary cause for a laggy response from applications, although sometimes the application itself could be flawed or buggy.

At the time of writing, less than 6% of all Android devices have Donut, Eclair, or Froyo versions. It is common for owners to upgrade to Gingerbread. As a result, Gingerbread accounts for more than 40% of the Android OS version distribution (Figure 2-1).

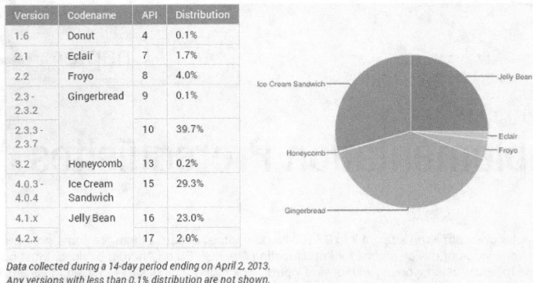

Version	Codename	API	Distribution
1.6	Donut	4	0.1%
2.1	Eclair	7	1.7%
2.2	Froyo	8	4.0%
2.3 - 2.3.2	Gingerbread	9	0.1%
2.3.3 - 2.3.7		10	39.7%
3.2	Honeycomb	13	0.2%
4.0.3 - 4.0.4	Ice Cream Sandwich	15	29.3%
4.1.x	Jelly Bean	16	23.0%
4.2.x		17	2.0%

Data collected during a 14-day period ending on April 2, 2013.
Any versions with less than 0.1% distribution are not shown.

Figure 2-1. Android OS: version distribution

> **Note**   The Android OS version distribution is available at http://developer.android.com/about/ dashboards/index.html, and Figure 2-1 provides a chart representing this.

Debuggable versions of heavy applications are slower than the optimized exported apk versions, and, if you are developing on pre-Gingerbread versions of Android, the garbage collector makes your application even slower (both debuggable and exported apk). There is no way to tackle this, since faster (concurrent) garbage collectors have only been available since Gingerbread. So, when beginning development of interactive graphics applications (based on ES 1.x or ES 2.0), be sure to do so on Gingerbread.

Choosing Inputs That Your Game Needs

Gameplay requires the use of inputs (or controls), through which the game logic comes to life. On handhelds, these inputs range from the basic UI (button-views, seekbars, touch, etc.) to motion and position sensors and peripherals. Although the gaming experience is enhanced by innovations, such as peripheral controls from controller manufacturers like Zeemote, game developers should attempt to minimize any need for external inputs (Figure 2-2 shows the Zeemote controller, which is coupled with the Android device via Bluetooth). Developers should even minimize (and optimize) the use of any UI that is natively available on Android handhelds, such as button-views and motion and position sensors. After all, a game for mobile devices becomes popular largely because it can be played anywhere and requires simply touching buttons on the screen, dragging a finger across the screen, or using sensors.

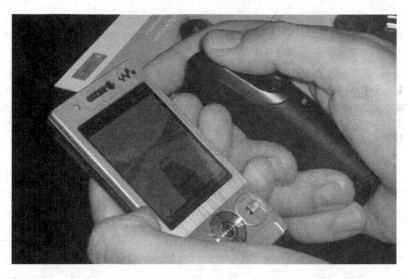

Figure 2-2. Zeemote JS1 game controller

Casual, Tower-Defense, and Puzzle games are the most popular genres of games on handhelds. In most of these games, the innovation and simplicity of the UI design (layout and use of visual elements, as well as the use of sensors) makes them widely accepted across all devices, by all groups of people, whether the game uses buttons to make a character jump or touch to position a basket and collect fruit (Figure 2-3).

Figure 2-3. Catchy Basket by MetaDesign Solutions Pvt Ltd

Simple UI designs in such games do not reflect limitations in the underlying hardware, since most Android devices offer powerful and feature-rich UIs. We just want the UI design to be as simple as it can be, in order to make the gameplay easy.

Although we have not yet discussed how to render graphics using ES 2.0, to develop an understanding of UI design (for gameplay inputs) I shall introduce a feature of 3D graphic rendering APIs called *3D-Transformation*. 3D-Transformation is the process of changing sizes, orientations, or positions of objects by mathematical operations, such as *Matrix Multiplication*. There are three types of 3D-Transformation:

- Geometric or Modeling transformation
- Coordinate or Viewing transformation
- Perspective or Projection transformation

At this stage, Geometric transformation (Modeling transformation) should be sufficient to better understand the game UI. Geometric transformation has three types:

- *Translation:* shifting an object to a new position
- *Scaling:* changing the dimensions of an object
- *Rotation:* rotating an object about a center

In Geometric transformation, an object is transformed to a new position (translation), a new size (scaling), or a new configuration (rotation). This transformation is achieved using matrices for various types of geometric transformation. Therefore, *translation* is achieved by using a *translate matrix*, *scaling* is achieved by using a *scale matrix*, and *rotation* is achieved by using a *rotate matrix*.

Note   It is possible to combine various transformations in a single matrix. For now, I do not want to expose you to advanced concepts. Chapter 3 demonstrates combining transformations, using Android's matrix math utilities.

Figure 2-4 shows a spacecraft trying to dodge incoming rocks. Assuming the image is a 3D scene in a game within which the motion of spacecraft is confined along the x and y axes, the only possible way to successfully dodge the rocks is by translating along the x-axis (in the directions in which the longer arrows are pointing). In graphic rendering APIs, this can only be achieved by translation transformation.

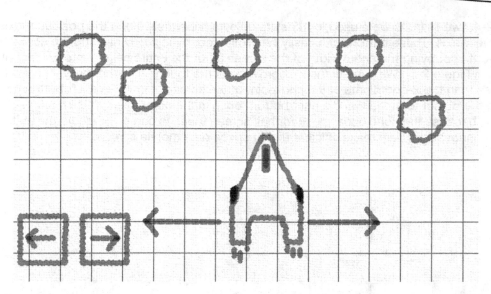

Figure 2-4. Translation using UI: Buttons

Graphic rendering APIs allow us to associate matrices with objects to animate them, and, for such a movement along the x-axis, APIs allow constant updating to the *translate matrix* associated with the object. For translation along the x-axis, we only need a measure of the (number of) moves along the x-axis. Hence, it should only require a UI design consisting of buttons for moves along the positive x-axis and the negative x-axis. Two buttons, one for left move and one for right move, are enough to dodge the incoming rocks in this case.

Note Throughout this book, we work in landscape mode, especially when working with game layout, so we can stay focused on one approach, instead of choosing between landscape and portrait modes. Moreover, landscape mode provides a wider view so UI elements, such as button-views and seekbars, can be widely laid out for a spacious look to the game.

Unlike gaming consoles, handhelds do not have controllers. Most games on handhelds use the screen to place the visual elements used as inputs for gameplay. Unlike the spacious screen of a tablet, space on a mobile screen is very limited. This is why we focus on the UI design on mobiles, rather than on tablets. Therefore, after designing the game UI, we need to reduce the area occupied by visual elements, such as button-views, to avoid cluttering UI and GPU rendered 3D graphics. You may wonder about the relationship between the rendering of game UI (visual elements like button-views and seekbars) and OpenGL's GPU rendering. Chapter 3 provides in-depth insight regarding that relationship. The examples in the following section, however, should help you understand the practical difference between game UI and OpenGL rendering.

In Figure 2-4, two buttons were used to translate objects separately along the positive x-axis and the negative x-axis. These buttons can easily be eliminated, by logically dividing the screen (or the widget layout occupying the entire width of the screen if not the entire height) into two equal parts (as shown in Figure 2-5). We can get the x-coordinate of the touch using MotionEvent.getX(). If this value is less than the x-coordinate of the mid-point of the screen, it imitates a left button touch for translating the object to the left, and a right button touch in the other case. This imitation is under our control, because the conditional block for half screen touches can now handle the matrix update code. Such innovations help make efficient use of space on a mobile screen.

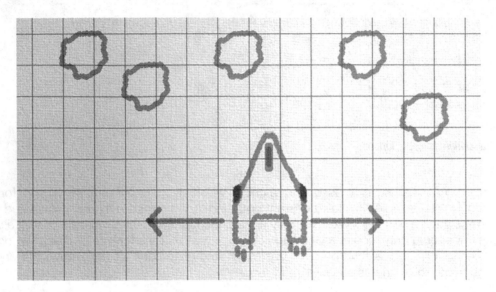

Figure 2-5. Translation using UI: Screen

Note   Every visual element (that inherits from View) in an Android application can be assigned a touch listener using the setOnTouchListener method. This method registers a listener for the callback method onTouch, which is invoked when a touch event is sent to this visual element. The onTouch method takes two arguments (of type View and MotionEvent). The View argument is for the view (visual element) that the touch event has been dispatched to, whereas the MotionEvent argument contains full information about the event (for example, the x and y coordinates of touch, which are accessed using the getX() and getY() methods of the MotionEvent class).

After translation, rotation is the most commonly used geometric transformation in games. Graphic rendering APIs allow us to associate rotation matrices with objects, just like the translation matrices. Like translation, rotation is implemented in a variety of ways. We can logically divide the screen for clockwise-anticlockwise spins, use buttons for spins, or use motion and position sensors to detect tilt (left-right) for different types of spins. In some cases, translation can be made automatic (a clever design principle becoming very common in popular modern games) so the screen can be used for rotation. This way, a lot of screen space can be left for a spacious look to the game.

Tank Fence

Having explained the necessary relationship between inputs for gameplay and object transformation (using graphic rendering APIs), it's time to introduce the game we will be working with.

This game is *Tank Fence*, a simple 3D shooting game in which the player gets to control a tank to guard a region against invaders. The UI for this game (Figure 2-6) consists of buttons for forward-backward movement of the tank, another button for firing weapons at the invaders, and touch (or optional use of motion and position sensors) to rotate the tank. The buttons intended for forward-backward movement will actually update the *translate matrix* we associate with the tank, and the touch (or optionally motion & position sensors) will update the *rotate matrix* used in combination with the *translate matrix*.

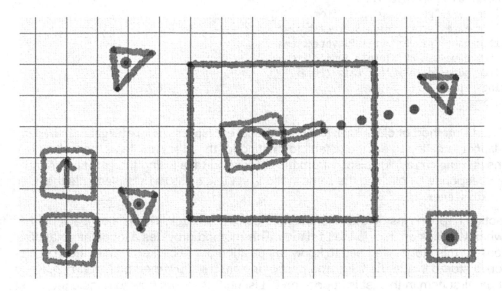

Figure 2-6. Tank Fence

We will start working on this game after discussing ES 2.0 fundamentals (*Buffers*, *GLSL*, *State Management* and *3D-Transformation*) in Chapter 3, and we will design the objects for the game (tank and invaders) using Blender in Chapter 4. But before that, let's see how to create menus for the game.

Creating Menus for the Game

Most games initialize with a main menu for options or settings, and the main menu displays after a splash screen, which is where the logo of the game is displayed. We won't use a splash screen, but I will explain the basic features and functioning of the *GAME MENU* application from the source code to help you get started with menus for the game.

Under "File Menu" in Eclipse, select "Import" and then select "Existing Projects into Workspace." Import the archive file gamemenu.zip from the *Chapter2* folder. This will load the *GAME MENU* application into your workspace.

Notice that the structure of the *GAME MENU* application is similar to the *GL SURFACE* application we created in Chapter 1. Unlike that application, however, we have a modified entry point; class Main in the Main.java file now extends the ListActivity class for hosting a ListView (with id @android:id/list) to display the menu options. The options are inside the options.xml file (Listing 2-1) inside the *res/values* folder.

Listing 2-1. GAME MENU/res/values/options.xml

```xml
<resources>
    <string-array name="options">
        <item name="game">New Game</item>
        <item name="score">High Score</item>
        <item name="player">Edit Player</item>
        <item name="sound">Toggle Sound</item>
        <item name="data">Clear Data</item>
    </string-array>
</resources>
```

In the onCreate method of class Main (GAME MENU/src/com/apress/android/gamemenu/Main.java), setListAdapter is called to set the default formatting for the ListView items, as well as to collect the options (string-array) for display from the options.xml file (using the getStringArray method). To initiate a response by clicking the items in the ListView, class Main implements the interface OnItemClickListener.

The real action happens inside the inherited method onItemClick. This is a callback method that is invoked when we click an item in the ListView. This method provides a lot of information about the clicked item. At this stage, we need to know the position of the clicked item in the ListView. This information is stored inside the third argument of the onItemClick method (int arg2). Keeping in mind that the first item in the list is at position 0, Listing 2-2 shows how to handle the clicks.

Listing 2-2. GAME MENU/src/com/apress/android/gamemenu/Main.java

```java
public void onItemClick(AdapterView<?> arg0, View arg1, int arg2, long arg3) {
 if (arg2 == 0) {
  startActivity(new Intent(Main.this, Game.class));
 }
 else if (arg2 == 1) {
  Dialog d = new Dialog(this);
  d.setContentView(R.layout.highscore);
  d.setTitle("High Score");
  d.show();
 }
```

```
else if (arg2 == 2) {
 Dialog d = new Dialog(this);
 d.setContentView(R.layout.editplayer);
 d.setTitle("Edit Player");
 d.show();
 }
}
```

Note   The *GAME MENU* application consists of default responses for handling most of the clicked items in the `ListView`. If you are an advanced Android developer, you can extend these responses later, but right now they are sufficient.

Since the list is displayed in the same order as the items inside the `options.xml` file (`string-array` in Listing 2-1 contains this list), it becomes easy to create `if` blocks to handle each clicked item according to its position in the list.

Inside the `if` block for "High Score" and "Edit Player" items (Listing 2-2), there are lines of code to invoke a dialog, which has some styling applied to it, which is defined in the *res/layout* folder. The `dimens.xml` and `strings.xml` files inside the *res/values* folder contain the padding-dimensions and the text (respectively) for the dialogs. Figures 2-7 and 2-8 show these dialogs.

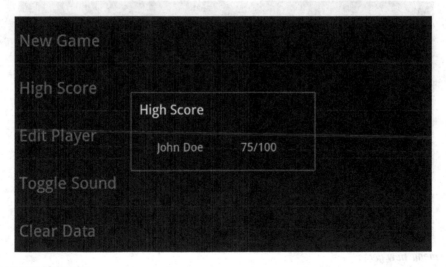

Figure 2-7. Game menu: high score

Figure 2-8. *Game menu: edit player*

When clicked, the "New Game" item starts a new activity to display an OpenGL surface view on the screen (Figure 2-9). The Java class for this new activity is identical to class Main from the *GL SURFACE* application; it has simply been renamed to Game. (The associated Renderer class for this activity is also identical to the GLES20Renderer class from the *GL SURFACE* application).

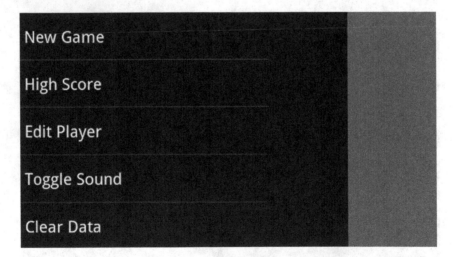

Figure 2-9. *Game menu: new game*

To make sure the *GAME MENU* application takes over the entire screen and is oriented in landscape mode, all the activity elements in the AndroidManifest.xml file must include the attributes and values shown in Listing 2-3. Table 2-1 provides the line descriptions for Listing 2-3.

Listing 2-3. GAME MENU/AndroidManifest.xml

```
android:configChanges="keyboard|keyboardHidden|orientation"
android:screenOrientation="landscape"
android:theme="@android:style/Theme.NoTitleBar.Fullscreen"
```

Table 2-1. Listing 2-3, lines description

Line	Description
1.	Hint Android to avoid performing the default reset of activity when the specified configurations change
2.	Set landscape orientation
3.	Make the activity full-screen

Now, we move on to an important topic to discuss using OpenGL views along with XML-based layouts and views.

Setting Views Using setContentView and addContentView

Activity content can be set to an explicit view using the setContentView method, which is a public method of the android.app.Activity class. Using this method, a View is placed directly into the activity's view hierarchy. This View can be as simple as a button-view (Listing 2-4, Figure 2-10) or it can itself be a complex view hierarchy, consisting of various layouts and views within it.

Listing 2-4. SETCONTENTVIEW/src/com/apress/android/setcontentview/Main.java

```java
@Override
public void onCreate(Bundle savedInstanceState) {
  super.onCreate(savedInstanceState);

  Button button = new Button(this);
  button.setText("SETCONTENTVIEW");
  setContentView(button);
}
```

> **Note**   Layout widgets, such as LinearLayout, as well as the widgets with visual representation, such as Button, (Listing 2-4) are all subclasses of the android.view.View class.

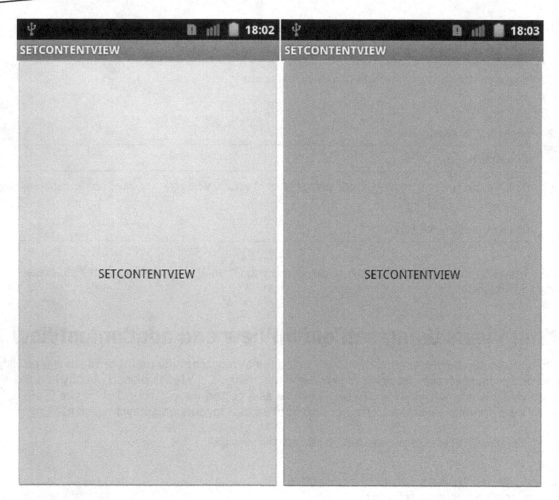

Figure 2-10. *setContentView with button-view*

We saw in Chapter 1 that the setContentView method can set an OpenGL surface as the activity's content view. This is possible because GLSurfaceView (android.opengl.GLSurfaceView) is a subclass of View.

On Android, all OpenGL rendering is hosted by GLSurfaceView. To modify this rendering using visual elements like button-views, we must separate them from GLSurfaceView. Android provides a convenient way to do so, using the addContentView method (addContentView(View view, LayoutParams params)).

The addContentView method is also a public method of the android.app.Activity class. Unlike the setContentView method, the addContentView method requires an extra argument to obtain the view's layout information.

Using the addContentView method, we add an additional content view to the activity. In an activity, if the argument passed to the setContentView method is an OpenGL surface and the first argument passed to the addContentView method is a layout widget, the OpenGL surface is laid out below the layout widget (Figure 2-11). To get a better understanding, let's create a new application:

1. Click the wizard to create a new Android project.

2. Set the application and project name as "ADDCONTENTVIEW."

3. Uncheck the "Create custom launcher icon" option and click "Next."

4. For "Create Activity," select BlankActivity and click "Next."

5. Set the "Activity Name" and "Layout Name" as "Main" and "main," respectively.

6. Click "Finish."

7. Copy the files GLES20Renderer.java and Main.java from *GL SURFACE* application into the package for *ADDCONTENTVIEW* application (confirm overwriting of Main.java).

setContentView(_surfaceView); in Main.java (*ADDCONTENTVIEW* application) sets an OpenGL surface as the activity's content view. Now, we add a layout widget (with button-views) as an additional content view (Listing 2-5).

Listing 2-5. ADDCONTENTVIEW/src/com/apress/android/addcontentview/Main.java

```
LinearLayout layout = new LinearLayout(this);
layout.setOrientation(LinearLayout.VERTICAL);
layout.setPadding(0, 200, 0, 0);
```

1. After line 16 (the line with the call to the setContentView method) in Main. java, add the lines of code from Listing 2-5 to create a LinearLayout layout with vertical orientation and top-padding of 200 pixels (if you are on Eclipse, you can quick fix errors to import the class android.widget.LinearLayout).

2. Create two buttons for this layout and name them "Up" and "Down," respectively.

3. After setting width and height for the buttons using setWidth and setHeight, set their layout parameters (Listing 2-6).

Listing 2-6. ADDCONTENTVIEW/src/com/apress/android/addcontentview/Main.java

```
Button buttonUp = new Button(this);
buttonUp.setText("Up");
buttonUp.setWidth(110);
buttonUp.setHeight(85);
LinearLayout.LayoutParams layoutParamsButtonUp = new LinearLayout.LayoutParams(
    LinearLayout.LayoutParams.WRAP_CONTENT,
    LinearLayout.LayoutParams.WRAP_CONTENT);
layoutParamsButtonUp.setMargins(0, 0, 0, 20);
```

```
Button buttonDown = new Button(this);
buttonDown.setText("Down");
buttonDown.setWidth(110);
buttonDown.setHeight(85);
LinearLayout.LayoutParams layoutParamsButtonDown = new LinearLayout.LayoutParams(
    LinearLayout.LayoutParams.WRAP_CONTENT,
    LinearLayout.LayoutParams.WRAP_CONTENT);
layoutParamsButtonDown.setMargins(0, 20, 0, 0);
```

> **Note**   If using Eclipse, do not forget to quick fix the errors.

4. Finally, add these buttons to the layout and add the layout widget as an additional content view using the addContentView method (Listing 2-7).

Listing 2-7. ADDCONTENTVIEW/src/com/apress/android/addcontentview/Main.java

```
layout.addView(buttonUp, layoutParamsButtonUp);
layout.addView(buttonDown, layoutParamsButtonDown);
layout.setGravity(Gravity.CENTER | Gravity.RIGHT);

addContentView(layout, new LayoutParams(LayoutParams.MATCH_PARENT,
    LayoutParams.MATCH_PARENT));
```

Using the addContentView method, visual elements like button-views are easily separated from the OpenGL rendering (Figure 2-11). This allows us to use OpenGL views along with XML-based layouts and views to conveniently control the 3D rendering on OpenGL surfaces using the UI.

Figure 2-11. OpenGL with XML/UI view

Note   Instead of writing Java code to create layout widgets with button-views, you can use
`LayoutInflater` to inflate XML-based layouts and views. The *ADDCONTENTVIEW INFLATER* application
(output seen in Figure 2-12) from the source code helps you get started with layout inflaters.

Figure 2-12. ADDCONTENTVIEW INFLATER application

Sleek Design of XML Views

Now, we make some changes to the *ADDCONTENTVIEW* application to give a sleek design to the
XML-based views, which we also use in the *Tank Fence* game:

1. In `Main.java`, clear all lines of code from the `onCreate` method after
    `setContentView(_surfaceView);`

    so the method body is reduced to:

    ```
    super.onCreate(savedInstanceState);
    surfaceView = new GLSurfaceView(this);
    surfaceView.setEGLContextClientVersion(2);
    surfaceView.setRenderer(new GLES20Renderer());
    setContentView(_surfaceView);
    ```

2. Add the lines of code from Listing 2-8 after the `setContentView` method to
    create a `LinearLayout` with `LayoutParams` `layoutParamsUpDown` and gravity
    bottom-left to keep the `LinearLayout` away from the back button while
    in landscape mode (we set `screenOrientation` to landscape later in this
    section). Quick fix errors (if any) to import the required classes.

Listing 2-8. SLEEK UI/src/com/apress/android/sleekui/Main.java

```
LinearLayout layout = new LinearLayout(this);
LinearLayout.LayoutParams layoutParamsUpDown = new LinearLayout.LayoutParams(
    LinearLayout.LayoutParams.MATCH_PARENT,
    LinearLayout.LayoutParams.MATCH_PARENT);
layout.setGravity(Gravity.BOTTOM | Gravity.LEFT);
```

3. To inflate XML-based views from a layout file, get access to the inflater service by calling: getSystemService(Context.LAYOUT_INFLATER_SERVICE);

4. Create a View object to reference the inflated view returned by the inflater.inflate method (as shown in Listing 2-9).

Listing 2-9. SLEEK UI/src/com/apress/android/sleekui/Main.java

```
LayoutInflater inflater = (LayoutInflater) getSystemService(Context.LAYOUT_INFLATER_SERVICE);
View linearLayoutView = inflater
    .inflate(R.layout.updown, layout, false);
```

5. After quick fixing the errors for unimported classes, rename the file main.xml (inside *res/layout* folder) as updown.xml.

6. Add the following string resources (Listing 2-10) to the strings.xml file (inside *res/values* folder):

Listing 2-10. SLEEK UI/res/values/strings.xml

```
<string name="up">UP</string>
<string name="down">DOWN</string>
```

7. Remove all lines from the updown.xml file and add the layout shown in Listing 2-11.

Listing 2-11. SLEEK UI/res/layout/updown.xml

```
<?xml version="1.0" encoding="utf-8"?>
<LinearLayout xmlns:android="http://schemas.android.com/apk/res/android"
    android:layout_width="wrap_content"
    android:layout_height="wrap_content"
    android:layout_marginBottom="5dp"
    android:layout_marginLeft="5dp"
    android:background="@android:drawable/alert_dark_frame"
    android:orientation="vertical"
    android:paddingBottom="11dp" >

    <Button
        android:layout_width="90dp"
        android:layout_height="wrap_content"
        android:layout_marginBottom="25dp"
        android:contentDescription="@string/app_name"
        android:text="@string/up" />
```

```
<Button
    android:layout_width="90dp"
    android:layout_height="wrap_content"
    android:contentDescription="@string/app_name"
    android:text="@string/down" />

</LinearLayout>
```

8. Add the inflated view (from 4) to the LinearLayout layout by calling layout. addView(linearLayoutView), then, add the layout as an additional content view by calling: addContentView(layout, layoutParamsUpDown);

The purpose of using the layout from Listing 2-11 is to ensure:

- *Wide buttons are used*: Buttons should have layout_width of 90dp (density independent pixels). Buttons should be at least that wide, because graphics applications, such as games, require users to interact continuously with UI elements, such as buttons, and, they are easy to click if wide enough.

- *LinearLayout does not get hidden*: Make sure the LinearLayout maintains a gap from the left corner of the screen and it has layout_marginLeft and layout_ marginBottom of 5dp.

- *Buttons have color contrast with other views*: By setting a dark background for LinearLayout using android:background="@android:drawable/alert_dark_ frame", it becomes easy to spot light-colored buttons, which helps quick interaction during gameplays. Use of layouts with border or background is a great way to debug your designs.

Be sure this activity takes the entire screen in landscape mode (as shown in Figure 2-13). Add the lines of code from Listing 2-3 to the activity element inside the manifest file for this application.

Figure 2-13. Landscape mode with UI

Working with Buttons and the Counter Class

Here, we finally discuss the functioning of an application that updates the rendering on an OpenGL surface using a layout (that we just created). To load that application into your workspace, import the archive file updowncounter.zip from the *Chapter2* folder.

Inside the *UPDOWN COUNTER* application (Figures 2-14 and 2-15), if you browse the *layout* folder, you will see the files updown.xml and counter.xml. The updown.xml file contains the layout from the previous topic. However, now the buttons contain ids "up" and "down" defined in the id.xml file (inside *res/values* folder), which also contains another id "counter," corresponding to the TextView inside the counter.xml file. The TextView (Figures 2-14 and 2-15) has some basic styling applied to it.

Buttons are assigned ids so they can be referenced from the Activity defined in Main.java file. This application contains the Renderer class from the previous application with slight modifications.

This application uses an important class Counter (this class will also be used in the *Tank Fence* game) to track the number of clicks on the up and down buttons. (The reasons for using synchronized blocks in this class are discussed in Chapter 3.) Let's see how this application works using the class Counter and GLES20Renderer:

- Each time a button is clicked, the static field _upDown (of class Counter) is modified by a call to getUpDownNextValue or getUpDownPreviousValue (called inside the click listeners for buttonUp and buttonDown).

- The glClearColor method (inside the GLES20Renderer class) takes float type arguments (in rgba format, in the 0 to 1 range) for coloring the entire OpenGL surface; hence, calling glClearColor(0.0f, 0.0f, 0.0f, 1); makes the entire screen black, as shown in Figure 2-14.

- The clearScreenWithColor method defined in the GLES20Renderer class takes an int type argument to modify the blue color component inside the glClearColor method.

- When the onDrawFrame method gets called (on refresh of the OpenGL surface), it invokes the clearScreenWithColor method by passing it the current value of the _upDown field (which is controlled by the buttons). This leads to a new color of the OpenGL surface each time the button is clicked (this will only happen if the blue color component is supplied a value in the 0 to 1 range).

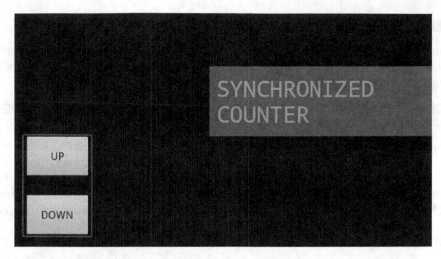

Figure 2-14. Synchronized counter application

This example gives you the basic idea of controlling the rendering on OpenGL surface by the use of UI like button-views (Figure 2-15).

Figure 2-15. Using buttons to affect the rendering

Similar to the technique used here, the following topics use touch and sensors in place of buttons to control graphic rendering on the OpenGL surface.

Take a closer look at the Counter class (UPDOWN COUNTER/src/com/apress/android/updowncounter/Counter.java) and the way it has been used with UI and Renderer. Understanding its usage is necessary to understand the concepts for using UI with OpenGL rendering.

Using Touch for Rotation

For the *Tank Fence* game, we implement rotation using the screen (or optionally using sensors). We won't use buttons for rotation. In this topic, you learn to use the screen using screen touch to update the *rotate matrix* associated with an object.

The *rotate matrix* associated with an object requires the desired angle of rotation (in degrees) to rotate the object by that angle about a particular axis.

If you want to use the screen to rotate an object about the axis perpendicular to it (the screen) so that the angle of rotation is proportional to the horizontal distance moved by a finger across the screen, take the ratio of the total horizontal distance moved to the width of the screen. For example, we can create a class that implements the interface OnTouchListener, and, inside the implemented method onTouch, we can use the code shown in Listing 2-12 to find the horizontal distance moved.

Listing 2-12. TOUCH ROTATION/src/com/apress/android/touchrotation/Main.java

```
if (event.getAction() == MotionEvent.ACTION_DOWN) {
 _touchedX = event.getX();
} else if (event.getAction() == MotionEvent.ACTION_MOVE) {
 float touchedX = event.getX();
 float dx = Math.abs(_touchedX - touchedX);
```

We get the device width by accessing the display metrics members, and we obtain the ratio of dx to the device width. We then convert this ratio into degrees, which can be used by the *rotate matrix* to rotate the object. This concept is utilized by the *TOUCH ROTATION* application (Figure 2-16), in the source code for this chapter. This application (via class Main) also takes into account the direction (left or right) in which the finger moves across the screen so as to handle clockwise and anticlockwise rotations separately.

To create such an application, we need two classes:

- *Renderer class:* to render an object as well as expose the *rotate matrix* (or related attributes like rotation angle) associated with this object

- *Main class:* to calculate the angle of rotation and update the *rotate matrix* using it

Load the *TOUCH ROTATION* application into your workspace. It contains both classes as described. You do not need to worry about the class GLES20Renderer at this stage; all that it does is:

- Renders a 3D object, which has a *rotate matrix* (_RMatrix) associated with it

- Exposes access to the field _zAngle, which stores the angle of rotation to update the *rotate matrix*

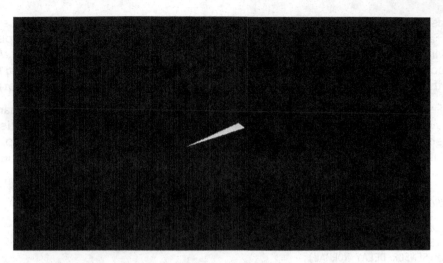

Figure 2-16. Rotating arrow with touch

The Main class implements a touch listener for calculating the ratio of the total horizontal distance moved to the width of the screen (inside its onTouch method). Because of the default sensitivity settings, if this ratio is 1/2, the object performs a complete rotation about the axis perpendicular to the screen. This class also contains if blocks to compare consecutive finger moves across the screen for clockwise and anticlockwise rotations (please note that the finger has to be lifted before the next swipe across the screen). The _TOUCH_SENSITIVITY and _filterSensitivity fields are used to make the rotations smooth. You can modify these fields to adjust the sensitivity of touch.

Rotation Using Android Sensors

Now we discuss the use of Android sensors as UI to update the 3D rendering on an OpenGL surface (Figures 2-17 to 2-21). Because of the varying support for sensors across various Android devices, we restrict the use of sensors to:

- *Accelerometer* (Motion sensor)
- *Gravity sensor* (Motion sensor)
- *Magnetometer* (Position sensor)

We access the sensors available on an Android device using the Android sensor API. This API helps us perform important sensor-related tasks on an Android handheld, such as determining the availability of a sensor, requesting raw sensor data, and registering sensor event listeners.

To get started with this API, create an instance of the sensor service, as shown in Listing 2-13.

Listing 2-13. SENSOR ROTATION/src/com/apress/android/sensorrotation/Main.java

```
SensorManager sm = (SensorManager) getSystemService(Context.SENSOR_SERVICE);
```

To create an instance of a specific sensor, use the class Sensor. The SensorManager class provides a method getDefaultSensor(int type) to access Sensor objects specified by the int type. However, we start receiving notifications for sensor events by registering a SensorEventListener. As in the application discussed in the previous section, the Main class for sensor application also implements a listener, but this time a SensorEventListener (android.hardware.SensorEventListener).

The interface SensorEventListener contains an important callback method onSensorChanged that provides the raw sensor data through the argument SensorEvent event. You may wonder how frequently SensorEvent reports new values. While registering a listener, we must also specify the delay or measurement rate for the listener. These rates are defined as static constants inside the SensorManager class (Listing 2-14).

Listing 2-14. SENSOR ROTATION/src/com/apress/android/sensorrotation/Main.java

```
sm.registerListener(this,
  sm.getDefaultSensor(Sensor.TYPE_ACCELEROMETER),
  SensorManager.SENSOR_DELAY_NORMAL);
sm.registerListener(this,
  sm.getDefaultSensor(Sensor.TYPE_MAGNETIC_FIELD),
  SensorManager.SENSOR_DELAY_NORMAL);
sm.registerListener(this, sm.getDefaultSensor(Sensor.TYPE_GRAVITY),
  SensorManager.SENSOR_DELAY_NORMAL);
```

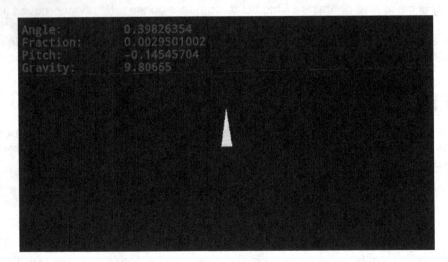

Figure 2-17. Rotating arrow using motion and position sensors

Apart from reporting raw sensor data, the SensorEvent object also lets us know about the accuracy of data returned, so we can stop processing the data if it cannot be trusted (Listing 2-15).

Using the getType method of the Sensor class, we can get information about the type of sensor that generated the sensor event. This allows our application to conveniently switch between sensors for obtaining different type of raw sensor data.

Listing 2-15. SENSOR ROTATION/src/com/apress/android/sensorrotation/Main.java

```java
public void onSensorChanged(SensorEvent event) {
 if (event.accuracy == SensorManager.SENSOR_STATUS_UNRELIABLE) {
  return;
 }

 switch (event.sensor.getType()) {
 case Sensor.TYPE_ACCELEROMETER: {
  _accelVals = event.values.clone();
  _accelValsFiltered[0] = _accelValsFiltered[0] * (1.0f - _a)
   + _accelVals[0] * _a;
  _accelValsFiltered[1] = _accelValsFiltered[1] * (1.0f - _a)
   + _accelVals[1] * _a;
  _accelValsFiltered[2] = _accelValsFiltered[2] * (1.0f - _a)
   + _accelVals[2] * _a;
  break;
 }
 case Sensor.TYPE_MAGNETIC_FIELD: {
  _magVals = event.values.clone();
  _magValsFiltered[0] = _magValsFiltered[0] * (1.0f - _a)
   + _magVals[0] * _a;
  _magValsFiltered[1] = _magValsFiltered[1] * (1.0f - _a)
   + _magVals[1] * _a;
  _magValsFiltered[2] = _magValsFiltered[2] * (1.0f - _a)
   + _magVals[2] * _a;
  break;
 }
 case Sensor.TYPE_GRAVITY: {
  _gravVals = event.values.clone();
  break;
 }
```

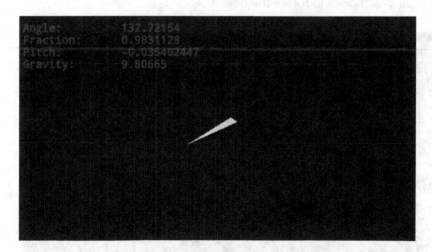

Figure 2-18. Rotating toward west through north (device facing up)

In Listing 2-15, the variables named _*Vals or _*Filtered are fields (float[3]) that store sensor data. They are multiplied with some (strange seeming) values to smooth the sensor data.

Finally, by calling the getRotationMatrix method (a public method of SensorManager class), the rotation matrix is computed, which can be directly used as a *rotate matrix* to rotate any 3D object rendered using OpenGL. Now, let's talk about the *SENSOR ROTATION* application from the source code for this chapter.

Like the *TOUCH ROTATION* application, the *SENSOR ROTATION* application contains a Renderer class for rendering a 3D object; and, once again, this class makes it possible to access the fields for rotating the object. However, class Main now implements the interface SensorEventListener to process the raw sensor data.

If you run this application on your Android device, you should see some text displayed in the top-left corner of the screen, because we have added a TextView as an additional content view. It is used to show:

- *Angle* of the object about the axis perpendicular to the screen (within an approximate range of -140° to 140°)

- *Fraction,* that is, extent of deviation from the mean position (within an approximate range of -1 to 1)

- *Pitch* or tilt about the longer edge of device (within an approximate range of -1 to 1)

- *Gravity* (within a range of 0 to 9.80665; it will never go beyond that range, even if testing this app inside a black hole!)

Because of some default settings in this application, when the object (arrow head) points along the positive y-axis (when the device is in landscape mode), east is indicated. This direction is the mean position of the object. *Angle* and *Fraction* are positive when the object points toward the left of mean position (Figure 2-18), and they are negative for the other case (Figure 2-19). We don't have to worry about *Pitch*; the *Angle* is sufficient to rotate the object.

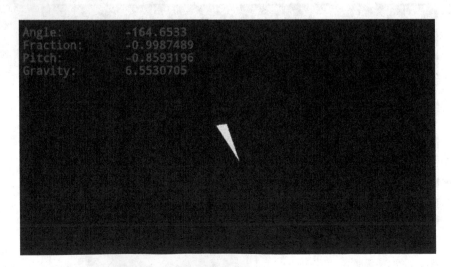

Figure 2-19. Rotating toward west through south (device facing up)

If you place your device flat on a surface and incline it, you should observe that, beyond a certain inclination, the rotation stops (Figures 2-20 and 2-21). The *SENSOR ROTATION* application contains this feature, because the object should only rotate when the device is held (almost) parallel to the surface.

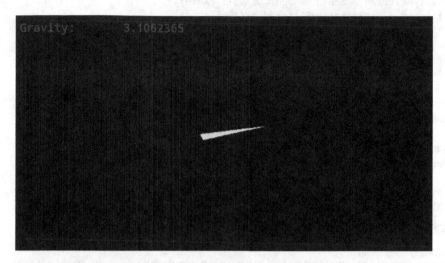

Figure 2-20. Stagnating rotation for large inclinations (Gravity 3.10)

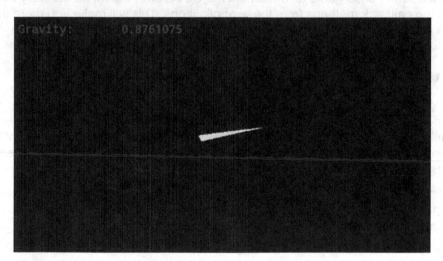

Figure 2-21. Stagnating rotation for large inclinations (Gravity 0.87)

To achieve this, the device is considered parallel only if _gravityFiltered is greater than or equal to 6. Inside the if block for handling this condition, there are lines of code to scale the angle of rotation (depending on the extent of inclination) to make it smooth. After scaling the angle, the results are displayed on a TextView (Listing 2-16).

Listing 2-16. SENSOR ROTATION/src/com/apress/android/sensorrotation/Main.java

```
if (_gravityFiltered >= 6
  && _gravityFiltered <= SensorManager.GRAVITY_EARTH * 1) {
 scaling = _SENSITIVITY
   + (2 - (_gravityFiltered / SensorManager.GRAVITY_EARTH));
 _orientationFiltered = _orientationFiltered * (1.0f - _a)
   + _outR[0] * _a;
 float zAngle = scaling * _orientationFiltered * 90;
 GLES20Renderer.setZAngle(zAngle);
 _textView.setText("Angle:          "
   + Float.valueOf(zAngle).toString() + "\n");
 _textView.append("Fraction:       "
   + Float.valueOf(_orientationFiltered).toString()
   + "\n");
 _textView.append("Pitch:          "
   + Float.valueOf(_values[1]).toString() + "\n");
 _textView
   .append("Gravity:        "
     + Float.valueOf(_gravityFiltered)
       .toString() + "\n");
}
```

The logic used in the *TOUCH ROTATION* and *SENSOR ROTATION* applications for obtaining inputs is also used in the *Tank Fence* game to implement the UI. So once again, go carefully through the class Main and the callback methods from these applications. This will make you more efficient with UI for applications.

Summary

At the beginning of this chapter I laid down some basic design principles for mobile game development in order to explain the role of sleek designs for our games. We then worked out a few examples to help you understand the practical differences between game UI and OpenGL rendering. Finally, we looked at the development of applications that update the rendering on OpenGL surfaces using the inputs obtained from buttons and sensors.

In the next chapter, you will learn about the OpenGL ES 2.0 environment on Android, and then we will create simple ES 2.0 applications to help us develop your understanding of the basic concepts of a programmable pipeline.

ES 2.0 Fundamentals

In the previous chapter you learned about the relationship between inputs for gameplay and transformations of OpenGL ES rendered graphics. I discussed the *Tank Fence* game and the functioning of *GAME MENU* application. Finally, we worked out methods to respond to events fired from button-views and sensors.

Here, in Chapter 3, we start working on ES 2.0 fundamentals, so we can render graphics using the GPU and resolve hardware accelerated graphic rendering details into a suitable form to teach the practical usage of OpenGL ES 2.0 API. My focus is on explaining programmable graphic rendering concepts, such as *GLSL*, through basic examples, rather than explaining object-oriented principles for creating an ES 2.0 application framework.

EGL on Android

EGL[1] is an interface between the native windowing system of an OS and the ES 2.0 API. It helps perform various important steps, from setting up a connection with (native) display to allowing the use of ES 2.0 functions. Fortunately on Android, most of the following steps are automatic:

1. *EGL initialization*, after its connection with the native display

2. *Selection of surface configuration* for various settings, such as the bit depth for color components

3. *EGL context creation* using the configuration in step 2

4. *"Make current" of context* for use with a rendering surface

5. *Addition of context* to an *EGL* window (that is, the rendering surface)

---

[1]http://en.wikipedia.org/wiki/EGL_(OpenGL)

The GLSurfaceView Class

The GLSurfaceView class (android.opengl.GLSurfaceView) performs this automation by managing *EGL*. Although most of the steps previously listed are automatic, step 2 requires you to specify the version of OpenGL ES you intend to use on your rendering surface by calling the setEGLContextClientVersion(int version) method, as shown in Listing 3-1.

Listing 3-1. GL SURFACE/src/com/apress/android/glsurface/Main.java

```
_surfaceView.setEGLContextClientVersion(2);
```

> **Note** There are other setEGL* methods you can use to configure the *EGL* context (for example, methods to configure the bit depth for RGB color components on the rendering surface); however, for all ES 2.0 applications used in this book, we have only made one configuration change by setting the version of OpenGL ES using setEGLContextClientVersion.

To use this class to render graphics on an *EGL* window (that is, the rendering surface), we first create an instance of type GLSurfaceView (android.opengl.GLSurfaceView), as shown in Listing 3-2. Then, we specify the version of OpenGL ES, so we can configure the current *EGL* context to become OpenGL ES 2.0 compatible.

Listing 3-2. GL SURFACE/src/com/apress/android/glsurface/Main.java

```
public class Main extends Activity {
 private GLSurfaceView _surfaceView;

 @Override
 public void onCreate(Bundle savedInstanceState) {
  super.onCreate(savedInstanceState);
  _surfaceView = new GLSurfaceView(this);
  _surfaceView.setEGLContextClientVersion(2);
  _surfaceView.setRenderer(new GLES20Renderer());
  setContentView(_surfaceView);
 }

}
```

> **Note** We have been calling the rendering surface different names—*EGL* window, OpenGL surface, OpenGL surface view, OpenGL view, and GL surface. Do not get confused; they are all the same.

Setting up the Renderer

Although the GLSurfaceView class can automate many steps, it cannot directly render graphics on the rendering surface. This requires a Renderer object that does the actual rendering. We specify the renderer using the setRenderer(GLSurfaceView.Renderer renderer) method. Abstract methods of the GLSurfaceView.Renderer interface (android.opengl.GLSurfaceView.Renderer) can be easily implemented within an anonymous inner type. However, for all ES 2.0 applications in the source code, we created a separate Renderer class—GLES20Renderer—similar to the Renderer class from the *GL SURFACE* application (Listing 3-3).

Listing 3-3. GL SURFACE/src/com/apress/android/glsurface/GLES20Renderer.java

```java
public class GLES20Renderer implements Renderer {

 public void onSurfaceCreated(GL10 gl, EGLConfig config) {
  GLES20.glClearColor(0.0f, 0.0f, 1.0f, 1);
 }

 public void onSurfaceChanged(GL10 gl, int width, int height) {
  GLES20.glViewport(0, 0, width, height);
 }

 public void onDrawFrame(GL10 gl) {
  GLES20.glClear(GLES20.GL_COLOR_BUFFER_BIT | GLES20.GL_DEPTH_BUFFER_BIT);
 }

}
```

After specifying the Renderer object, add this surface to the view hierarchy of the current activity using the setContentView method discussed in Chapter 2.

Renderer Thread

Using the GLSurfaceView class and the addContentView method, we can conveniently decouple OpenGL ES graphics from XML-based views (discussed in Chapter 2, section "Setting Views Using setContentView and addContentView"), so that the XML-based views get displayed on top of the rendering surface hosting the 3D graphics (as shown in Figure 3-1).

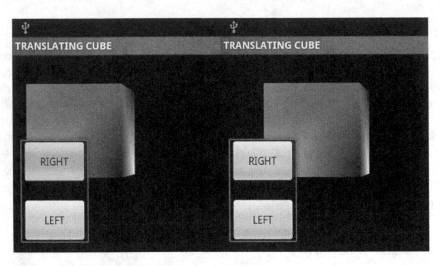

Figure 3-1. Decoupling of OpenGL ES graphics from XML-based views

Decoupling for Dedicated Performance

This decoupling is not restricted to a "physical" sense. Behind the scenes, the GLSurfaceView class (via Renderer object) renders the OpenGL ES graphics on a separate thread to dissociate any rendering functionality from the UI/main thread. This helps to avoid the cramming of UI thread with various ES 2.0 calls, and, while 3D graphics are rendered on a dedicated thread, Android can still maintain the UI thread to receive events from XML-based views, as well as sensors. We call this dedicated thread our renderer thread.

> **Note**   In the Android sensor API, the callback method onSensorChanged requests data in an asynchronous manner, so the UI thread is not blocked while waiting for a piece of data.

We can use standard Java techniques (Thread class/Runnable interface) to communicate between the UI and renderer thread. However, for all the examples in the source code in which we have to update the rendering based on inputs received from UI, we have only used static field(s) in various classes to share data between these two threads. To ensure thread safety while the static field is being accessed, we used either the volatile keyword with static field or the synchronized block.

Thread Safety

When multiple threads access a static field:

1.   Each thread may cache the field's value locally; as a result, when we read its value from a thread (after it is updated), an old value can be read. To avoid this, the static field is marked as volatile (this has been used in the *TOUCH ROTATION* and *SENSOR ROTATION* applications). This forces the thread to read the global value of the field.

2. Threads might attempt to update the field simultaneously; as a result, a race condition may arise, leading to an undesired value of the field. To avoid this, a static object can be synchronized (as shown in the *UPDOWN COUNTER* application) to ensure only one thread gets into the synchronized block (at a given time).

Using static field(s) to share data is only an alternative to standard Java techniques for cross-thread communication. We leave out the standard Java techniques to keep you away from multithreading; we want to focus on ES 2.0 fundamentals on Android. For most of our examples, the alternatives suffice, because, out of the two threads (UI/main thread and renderer thread), only the former is updating the static field(s).

Implemented Methods

The GLSurfaceView class requires a renderer that does the actual rendering; it is specified using the setRenderer(GLSurfaceView.Renderer renderer) method. In the following sections, we talk more about the abstract methods—onSurfaceCreated, onSurfaceChanged, and onDrawFrame—inherited by the class GLES20Renderer, which implements the interface GLSurfaceView.Renderer.

Anatomy of a Renderer

While creating the *GL SURFACE* application in Chapter 1, we intentionally sorted the methods of the class GLES20Renderer in a specific order. We did so to signify the actual sequence in which these methods get called. To understand this, we create an application similar to *GL SURFACE*, but before that, let's discuss Listing 3-4 - pseudo code to describe the internal functioning of a renderer thread (after GLSurfaceView is set as the activity's content view, as shown in Listing 3-2).

Listing 3-4. High Level Overview of Renderer Thread's Functioning

```
// after setContentView(_surfaceView);
_surfaceView.draw() { // there is no such method actually
 Renderer.surfaceCreated();
 Renderer.surfaceChanged(_width, _height);

 while(true) {
  Renderer.drawFrame();
  if(_deviceOrientationChanged) {
   _surfaceView.draw();
   break;
  }
  if(_stopped) {
   return;
  }
 }
}
```

Rendering begins with a call to the Renderer.surfaceCreated (that is, Renderer.onSurfaceCreated) method. Inside this method, we can place ES 2.0 functions for rendering graphics using the GPU.

However, the surfaceCreated method is the block in which we usually add code for basic *State Management* apart from setting the background color for our rendering surface.

To accommodate any change in the orientation of device, the surfaceChanged (that is, Renderer.onSurfaceChanged) method is called.

To render graphics on a frame by frame basis, the call to the Renderer.drawFrame (that is, Renderer.onDrawFrame) method takes place inside a while loop, which ends only if the application (or the activity using the rendering surface) is stopped.

Inside this loop, as soon as any orientation change is detected, _surfaceView begins the rendering again, starting from the surfaceCreated method.

Listing 3-4 is an attempt to approximately describe the internal functioning of a renderer thread (after an OpenGL surface view has been set as the activity's content view). However, it is clear enough to help understand the use of abstract methods implemented by the GLES20Renderer class.

GL SURFACE CHANGED Application

Now, we create an application to test whether these methods get called in the order we specified in the *GL SURFACE* application. To do so, create a new Android application *GL SURFACE CHANGED*, and set the "Activity Name" to "Main." Then, copy the files Main.java and GLES20Renderer.java from *GL SURFACE* into the package folder for this application (Eclipse will warn you that Main.java exists in the selected destination; confirm overwriting of Main.java).

Modify the GLES20Renderer class by adding the line of code shown in Listing 3-5 to its onSurfaceCreated method.

Listing 3-5. GL SURFACE CHANGED/src/com/apress/android/glsurfacechanged/GLES20Renderer.java

```
Log.d("onSurfaceCreated","invoked");
```

We have not yet imported the Log class. Quick fix the error to import this class. Although there are various methods we can use to log messages to the *LogCat* view (for example, Log.v and Log.i), we have used the d method to log a debug message.

Add lines similar to Listing 3-5 in the remaining methods, so the Renderer class becomes similar to Listing 3-6.

Listing 3-6. GL SURFACE CHANGED/src/com/apress/android/glsurfacechanged/GLES20Renderer.java

```
public class GLES20Renderer implements Renderer {

 public void onSurfaceCreated(GL10 gl, EGLConfig config) {
  GLES20.glClearColor(0.0f, 0.0f, 1.0f, 1);
  Log.d("onSurfaceCreated","invoked");
 }

 public void onSurfaceChanged(GL10 gl, int width, int height) {
  GLES20.glViewport(0, 0, width, height);
  Log.d("onSurfaceChanged","invoked");
 }
```

```
public void onDrawFrame(GL10 gl) {
 GLES20.glClear(GLES20.GL_COLOR_BUFFER_BIT | GLES20.GL_DEPTH_BUFFER_BIT);
 Log.d("onDrawFrame","invoked");
 }

}
```

When you run this application on your Android device, you see an OpenGL surface (Figure 3-2) like the one we created in Chapter 1. If you change your device's orientation, the OpenGL surface rearranges itself to fit the new orientation.

Figure 3-2. GL SURFACE CHANGED application in portrait mode

Note   Before you run this application, make sure you did not include the attributes (android:configChanges and android:screenOrientation) and values given in Listing 2-3 to the activity element of your manifest file.

After changing the device's orientation, exit the application. Next, open the *LogCat* view in Eclipse and add a filter text:invoked, as shown in Figure 3-3. This allows us to spot the debug messages we logged using Listing 3-6.

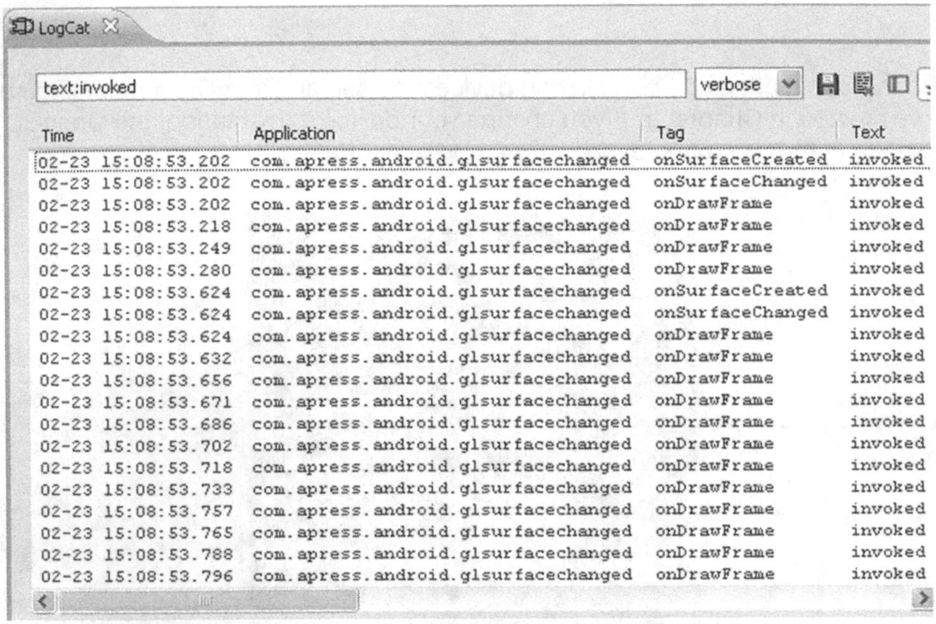

Figure 3-3. LogCat view, filtering log by text

If you look at the debug messages in the *LogCat* view, you will see that the messages are in an order similar to that in Figure 3-3. As mentioned, rendering begins with a call to the onSurfaceCreated method. Then the onSurfaceChanged method gets called to accommodate any change in orientation, and both of these methods are called again if we change the device's orientation. The onDrawFrame method is always called (repeatedly) after these two.

You can also make changes to the manifest file for this application to see what happens when the attributes and values given in Listing 2-3 are added to the activity element. When you run the application after making these changes, you will see a modifed order of debug messages in the *LogCat* view.

Although I talked about the purpose of abstract methods inherited by the GLE20Renderer class, I did not mention anything about the arguments passed to those methods. The only arguments that matter here are the int width and int height arguments, which are passed to the onSurfaceChanged method. The following section discusses the use of width and height arguments.

Until now, we have been addressing the OpenGL ES 2.0 environment on Android, as well as how ES 2.0 is invoked inside our activity. The following sections introduce the core concepts of the OpenGL ES 2.0 API, and we create basic examples to see ES 2.0 in action.

Framebuffer

When rendering graphics using ES 2.0, what we finally see in the *EGL* window (that is, the rendering surface) is colored pixels. There has to be a piece of memory that stores this data (color per pixel), so it can be displayed on the *EGL* window. Framebuffer is that large piece of memory used to represent 3D graphics as a 2D array of pixel data, more specifically, the kind of framebuffer we are talking about is a color buffer. Display devices read the color buffer to determine the intensity values for RGB color components for each pixel on the screen (that is, a portion of screen displaying the *EGL* window). Please note that the color buffer can also store an additional alpha component along with the RGB color components for each pixel on the *EGL* window.

In the section "EGL on Android", I mentioned that the GLSurfaceView class automates the selection of surface configuration for rendering surface. Let's elaborate a bit on that.

The default surface configuration that the GLSurfaceView class selects is *RGB_565*. This means that the memory allocated for each element (corresponding to a pixel on the *EGL* window) in the color buffer is 16 bits, where 5 bits are allocated for each red and blue color components, and 6 bits for the green color component (because the human visual system is more sensitive to green). We will stick to this default configuration (please note that the newer Android devices have this default configuration as *RGB_888*).

> **Note** A pixel (originally short for "picture element") is a minute, uniquely identifiable illuminated region on the display screen. It is not the smallest element on the display screen. The display device has the responsibility to determine what should be the smallest addressable screen element; however, these elements are way too small to be noticed individually, which is why they are combined in groups to form pixels.

Double Buffering

Based on what we've discussed so far, you might think that, when we update OpenGL ES graphics using the Renderer class (on a frame by frame basis), we only affect a single color buffer associated with the *EGL* window. However, when we render graphics on the *EGL* window, we actually update the "back" color buffer associated with it, and, when rendering gets completed, this buffer is swapped with a "front" color buffer. For this reason, the color buffer is said to be **double buffered** (please note that the swapping of buffers must be in sync with the refresh rate of the display screen). Double buffering is necessary to ensure that the displayable "front" color buffer is not being updated while the display device is reading it.

> **Note** As we have seen, various steps are automatically taken care of in the background so we can easily use OpenGL ES on Android. Once again, Android takes the burden away from us and manages the swapping of "front" and "back" color buffers via the GLSurfaceView class.

Clearing the Color Buffer

Before we start rendering graphics on the *EGL* window, we have to clear the (associated) color buffer with a specific color. We do this by calling the GLES20.glClear method and passing it an argument GLES20.GL_COLOR_BUFFER_BIT (since Android API level 8, you can access OpenGL ES 2.0 constants and functions using the class android.opengl.GLES20). Because we render graphics on a frame by frame basis, the glClear method is called inside the onDrawFrame method. This ensures that the color buffer is cleared with a default color before it is updated with pixel data from graphics rendered using OpenGL ES. To set this default color, we must call the glClearColor method prior to calling the glClear method. Using the glClearColor method, we specify the color value (in the range [0, 1]) that all elements in the color buffer should be initialized to. As you saw in the *GL SURFACE* application in Chapter 1, the clear color was set to (0.0, 0.0, 1.0, 1.0) so the screen was cleared to blue. Please note that, although the glClear method is usually called inside the onDrawFrame method, the glClearColor method is called inside the onSurfaceCreated method.

> **Note**   We used the glClear method in almost all applications so far, but the argument we usually passed (like, in *GL SURFACE* application) was different from what we discussed in this topic. This was done intentionally, so you get into the habit of using the code snippet shown in Listing 3-7; there would be no change in the output if we removed the extra part (| GLES20.GL_DEPTH_BUFFER_BIT) from the argument.

Listing 3-7. GL SURFACE CHANGED/src/com/apress/android/glsurfacechanged/GLES20Renderer.java

```
GLES20.glClear(GLES20.GL_COLOR_BUFFER_BIT | GLES20.GL_DEPTH_BUFFER_BIT);
```

Setting the Viewport

When the display device accesses "front" color buffer to display a final image of the graphics rendered using OpenGL ES, it needs to know about the viewport - that is, the area on the display screen on which this image is to be mapped.

We set the viewport using the glViewport(int x, int y, int width, int height) method, where (x, y) is a position on the display screen, measured from its bottom-left corner (in pixels). The rest of the arguments are for setting the size of viewport in pixels. To ensure the viewport is visible, (x, y) should lie within the bottom-left (x=0, y=0) and top-right (x=width, y=height) corners of the display screen.

We typically want the viewport to be the same size as the display screen (Figure 3-4). So, while setting the size of the viewport, we make use of the int width and int height arguments of the onSurfaceChanged method. These arguments store the width and height of the display screen in any orientation. For this reason, we need to call the glViewport method inside the onSurfaceChanged method. Whenever the orientation of the device changes, the onSurfaceChanged method helps keep track of the new width and height of the display screen in landscape or portrait orientations.

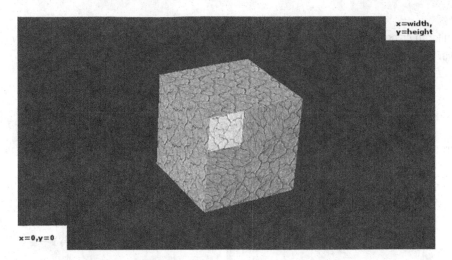

Figure 3-4. Rendering graphics on the entire screen

Figures 3-4 and 3-5 are screen shots from the *GL CUBEMAP TEXTURE* application (inside the source code for Chapter 5). Figure 3-4 shows the screen shot for the default viewport setting - that is, glViewport(0, 0, width, height). This setting fits the viewport on the display screen exactly.

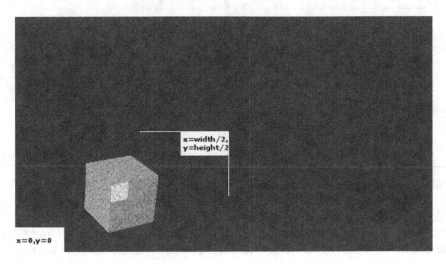

Figure 3-5. Setting the viewport as one-fourth of screen area

By calling glViewport(0, 0, width/2, height/2); the viewport area is reduced to a quarter of the display screen, as shown in Figure 3-5. You can modify the viewport settings for any of the application discussed, and you can try to shift the viewport at various positions on the display screen. If you set the viewport smaller than the display screen, you will still see the clear color (specified using glClearColor) in the area outside viewport. This is so because the call to the glClear method is unaffected by the call to the glViewport method. Therefore, regardless of viewport area, the rest of the display screen also gets colored.

> **Note** Similar to color buffer, there is another kind of framebuffer associated with the *EGL* window, which is discussed in the final section of this chapter.

GLSL

Finally, we can start the discussion on *GLSL*, but please note that, for all examples we work with in this topic, we restrict their rendering to two dimensions (as shown in Figure 3-6), because we haven't yet discussed OpenGL ES coordinate systems.

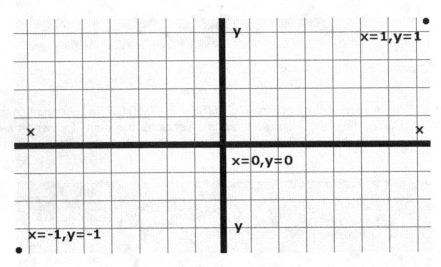

Figure 3-6. Normalized 2D space

GLSL (OpenGL Shading Language) is a graphics programming language that enables us to create *shader programs* to perform rendering effects in a flexible manner. These programs are a part of the programmable rendering pipeline that does not comprise of hard-coded functions to achieve transformation, lighting, and texturing effects. The *OpenGL Architecture Review Board* (*ARB*) created GLSL to provide an intuitive method for programming the rendering pipeline at the *vertex* and *fragment* levels. Embedded devices, such as mobiles and tablets, support the OpenGL ES Shading Language (also known as *GLSL ES* or *ESSL*), which is based on *GLSL* version 1.20.

Please note that, from this point, unless we need to talk about the comparison between *GLSL* and *GLSL ES*, we will refer to the latter as *GLSL*.

> **Note** In 3D computer graphics, the terms graphics pipeline or rendering pipeline most commonly refer to the method of converting a 3D scene (as a collection of points, lines, and polygons), which is supported by the graphics hardware, into a 2D "raster" image (that is, a collection of pixels or dots) as output. OpenGL and Direct3D are the most popular 3D graphic rendering APIs, both describing very similar graphic pipelines.
>
> Understanding various stages in the graphics pipeline can be overwhelming for new graphics developers. So, we don't discuss each explicitly. However, in the context of *GLSL*, we surely understand two programmable stages in the ES 2.0 graphics pipeline.

Shader Program

Shader programs (or simply, *shaders*) are computer programs to control the functionality of graphics pipeline in "programmable" 3D graphic rendering APIs, such as OpenGL ES 2.0. *GLSL* allows us to create two types of *shaders*:

- *Vertex shader*
- *Fragment shader*

The most interesting fact about the ES 2.0 rendering pipeline is that no object can be rendered on the OpenGL surface until a (valid) vertex and fragment shader have been created. Don't think you can get away with a "dot" on the OpenGL surface! Rendering a point also requires a vertex and fragment shader.

A vertex shader takes the geometry data, such as vertices in 3D space, of an object and transforms this data to the 2D coordinates at which it appears on the display screen. Then the rendering pipeline generates appropriate fragments for this object, which are then processed by a fragment shader for coloring, lighting, and/or texturing of the object (as shown in Figure 3-9).

> **Note** Each fragment represents a pixel (x, y) on the display screen that is yet to be processed by a fragment shader for coloration.

Finally, the fragment data is stored in a framebuffer to provide color values for those pixels on the display screen that represent this object. Simply, a vertex shader defines the final position of an object on the display screen (as a collection of vertices), as shown in Figure 3-7, whereas a fragment shader defines the final color of pixels that are filled by this object (Figure 3-9).

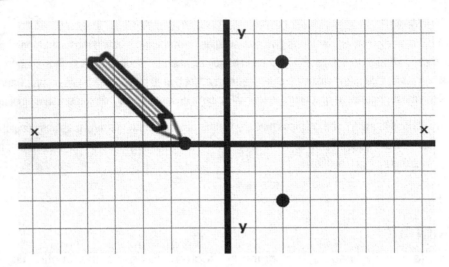

Figure 3-7. Vertex marking

Vertex Shader Example

Now, we discuss a vertex shader (written using *GLSL*) to define a point. As you know, a renderer specified using the setRenderer(GLSurfaceView.Renderer renderer) method actually renders graphics on the OpenGL surface. We usually create *shaders* directly inside this renderer (GLES20Renderer class) as literal strings (Listing 3-8).

Listing 3-8. GL POINT BASIC/src/com/apress/android/glpointbasic/GLES20Renderer.java

```
private final String _pointVertexShaderCode =
  "void main() {"
+ " gl_PointSize = 15.0;"
+ " gl_Position = vec4(0.0,0.0,0.0,1);"
+ "}";
```

The syntax of *shaders* is similar to that of the C programming language. If you can read and understand a simple C program, you will quickly grasp the basic structure of *shaders*.

GLSL shaders have a single entry point, called the *main* function, as shown in Listing 3-8. Additionally, they have built-in variables to provide useful information to the rendering pipeline. The point vertex shader (_pointVertexShaderCode) in Listing 3-8 makes use of two important built-in variables—gl_PointSize and gl_Position.

As the name suggests, gl_PointSize specifies the size of a "point" in pixels. This built-in variable can only be used with a specific type of geometric object in ES 2.0—a **point sprite**.

In ES 2.0, any object (for example, triangle, square, and cube) rendered on the OpenGL surface can only be expressed as a combination of any one of the following fundamental geometric objects (known as **primitives**):

■ **Point sprite**

■ **Line**

■ **Triangle**

We describe a primitive by a set of vertices (a single vertex in case of one **point sprite**, two vertices for a **line**, and three vertices for a **triangle**) and optional data for colors and textures. The vertex shader shown in Listing 3-8 is for rendering a point sprite primitive; this primitive is a square shaped point, and, as already stated, we specify its size using the gl_PointSize built-in.

Note   You may wonder exactly how we specify the type of primitive(s) we intend to render on the OpenGL surface. We do this inside the onDrawFrame method, using ES 2.0 functions—glDrawArrays or glDrawElements. These functions take primitive-type (GL_POINTS, GL_LINES, or GL_TRIANGLES) as an argument. We deal with glDrawArrays within this section.

---

gl_Position is a special built-in variable. If the vertex shader does not write to it, the graphics pipeline won't know of the vertex (of an object) we intend to render on the OpenGL surface. Considering the OpenGL world is similar to Figure 3-6, when we set gl_Position as vec4(0.0, 0.0, 0.0, 1), we define a point at the center of OpenGL surface (Figure 3-8). You may have understood already that vec4 is a four-component vector (not to be confused with the physical quantity "vector"), representing a 3D point in the OpenGL world. The last component in the vector vec4(0.0, 0.0, 0.0, 1) does not represent any visualizable quantity. It is added as a practical tool to enable matrix multiplications for various 3D-Transformations (you can read more about this at http://stackoverflow.com/a/2465290). If this vec4 were to represent a "vector" quantity (not a 3D point), then, in place of '1,' we have to append '0' as the last component.

Figure 3-8. Point sprite

Data Types

Like regular C types, the following basic types are commonly used in *GLSL*:

- *void:* used with functions that do not return a value or for an empty argument list
- *bool:* represents boolean values true or false
- *int:* a single signed integer
- *float:* a single floating-point scalar

Vectors with two, three, or four components are also available for the basic types mentioned previously:

- *bvec2:* a boolean vector of two components
- *bvec3:* a boolean vector of three components
- *bvec4:* a boolean vector of four components
- *ivec2:* an integer vector of two components
- *ivec3:* an integer vector of three components
- *ivec4:* an integer vector of four components
- *vec2:* a floating-point vector of two components
- *vec3:* a floating-point vector of three components
- *vec4:* a floating-point vector of four components

Apart from these, we can also construct square matrices—`mat2`, `mat3` and `mat4`—from scalars, vectors, or a combination of both scalars and vectors. Matrices are very useful data types, because they can be associated with objects to transform them by updating the 3D-Transformation data, such as the amount of translation and angle of rotation.

Now we'll look at some examples of declaring and initializing variables of various types using *GLSL*. For these examples, we modify Listing 3-8 in such a way that the output of the point vertex shader is not affected.

> **Note**   Apart from creating *shaders* as string literals, we can also create them in separate files. However, since we create *shaders* directly inside the `GLES20Renderer` class (as string literals), we must append some lines of *shaders* with "\n." We only do this for lines that contain single line comments or preprocessor directives (yes, *GLSL* supports comments and preprocessor directives).
>
> For most ES 2.0 applications in the source code, you will observe that all lines of *shaders* are appended with "\n." This has been done for readability purposes only, but you should understand which lines necessarily require "\n."

In Listing 3-9, instead of directly assigning the value '15.0' to gl_PointSize variable, another variable pointSize is declared and initialized. Its value is assigned to gl_PointSize variable using gl_PointSize = pointSize.

Listing 3-9. GL POINT BASIC/src/com/apress/android/glpointbasic/GLES20Renderer.java

```
private final String _pointVertexShaderCode =
  "void main() {"
+ " // declare & initialize float scalar \n"
+ " float pointSize = 15.0;"
+ " gl_PointSize = pointSize;"
+ ""
+ " // using vec3 constructor \n"
+ " vec3 xyz;"
+ " xyz = vec3(0.0,0.0,0.0);"
+ ""
+ " // using vec4 constructor \n"
+ " vec4 position;"
+ " position = vec4(xyz[0],xyz[1],xyz[2],1);"
+ " gl_Position = position;"
+ "}";
```

A three-component vector, named "xyz," is first declared, and then it is initialized using vec3 constructor vec3(0.0, 0.0, 0.0). One way to access the components of vectors is using the subscript "[]" operator and the indexing is zero-based, so xyz[0] corresponds to the first component of this vector. As shown in Listing 3-9, components of the xyz vector initialize the variable named "position," which is of type vec4. The last component of "position" is set to '1', and, finally, its value is assigned to the gl_Position variable.

Listing 3-10 demonstrates the use of **component names**. Depending on the number of components that make up a given vector, each component can be accessed through the component names {x, y, z, w}, {r, g, b, a}, or {s, t, r, q}. To access the individual components, first use the "." operator with the vector name, followed by the component name. However, please note that we cannot mix the component naming conventions when accessing a vector; only one convention is used at a time—vec4(xyz.x, xyz.y, xyz.z, 1).

Listing 3-10. GL POINT BASIC/src/com/apress/android/glpointbasic/GLES20Renderer.java

```
private final String _pointVertexShaderCode =
  "void main() {"
+ " gl_PointSize = 15.0;"
+ ""
+ " // declare & initialize vec3 vector \n"
+ " vec3 xyz = vec3(0.0,0.0,0.0);"
+ ""
+ " // declare & initialize vec4 vector \n"
+ " vec4 position = vec4(xyz.x,xyz.y,xyz.z,1);"
+ " gl_Position = position;"
+ "}";
```

Finally, in Listing 3-11, you see another style of using a vector constructor. If we pass a single scalar argument to a vector constructor, its value is used to set all values of the vector. So, using vec3(0.0) produces the same result as using vec3(0.0, 0.0, 0.0). We can also pass a vector as an argument to a vector constructor. Since the components of a vector are set from left to right (when using a vector constructor), vec4(vector3Name, 1) is identical to vec4(vector3Name.x, vector3Name.y, vector3Name.z, 1).

Listing 3-11. GL POINT BASIC/src/com/apress/android/glpointbasic/GLES20Renderer.java

```
private final String _pointVertexShaderCode =
  "void main() {"
+ " gl_PointSize = 15.0;"
+ ""
+ " // using vec3 constructor \n"
+ " vec3 xyz = vec3(0.0);"
+ ""
+ " // using vec4 constructor \n"
+ " vec4 position = vec4(xyz,1);"
+ " gl_Position = position;"
+ "}";
```

Fragment Shader Example

Continuing the vertex shader example for the point sprite primitive, we discuss a fragment shader (Listing 3-12) to define the final color of fragment for this primitive.

Listing 3-12. GL POINT BASIC/src/com/apress/android/glpointbasic/GLES20Renderer.java

```
private final String _pointFragmentShaderCode =
  "void main() {"
+ " gl_FragColor = vec4(1.0,1.0,1.0,1);"
+ "}";
```

Like the vertex shader, the fragment shader also contains a special built-in variable—gl_FragColor. The fragment shader needs to write to this variable to define the final color of a fragment. As shown in Figure 3-8, the color of the point sprite is set to white by assigning the value vec4(1.0, 1.0, 1.0, 1), representing RGBA color, to the gl_FragColor variable.

If you understood the examples shown, to declare and initialize variables in *GLSL* (Listings 3-9 to 3-11), you may want to experiment with Listing 3-12 to change how vec4 is written to the gl_FragColor variable (Listing 3-13):

Listing 3-13. GL POINT BASIC/src/com/apress/android/glpointbasic/GLES20Renderer.java

```
private final String _pointFragmentShaderCode =
  "void main() {"
+ " vec4 fragColor = vec4(1.0);"
+ " // i.e. fragColor = vec4(1.0,1.0,1.0,1.0); \n"
+ " gl_FragColor = fragColor;"
+ "}";
```

Although everything is fine in Listing 3-13, this code will not produce the intended result shown in Figure 3-8, because there is an important difference between a vertex and fragment shader. To be specific, you will get a blank screen if you replace the fragment shader code in the Renderer class in *GL POINT BASIC* application with Listing 3-13.

In *GLSL*, variables of type int or float must specify precision qualifiers. Precision qualifiers allow us to specify the precision with which computations for a *shader* variable are performed. Variables can be declared to have low, medium, or high precision, which is specified using keywords **lowp**, **mediump**, or **highp**, respectively. The default precision qualifier is specified at the top of a vertex or fragment shader (Listing 3-14):

- precision mediump float;

- precision mediump int;

Listing 3-14. GL POINT BASIC/src/com/apress/android/glpointbasic/GLES20Renderer.java

```
private final String _pointFragmentShaderCode =
  "#ifdef GL_FRAGMENT_PRECISION_HIGH \n"
+ "precision highp float;"
+ "#else \n"
+ "precision mediump float;"
+ "#endif \n"
+ "void main() {"
+ " vec4 fragColor = vec4(1.0);"
+ " gl_FragColor = fragColor;"
+ "}";
```

The precision specified for float will be used as the default precision for all variables based on a floating-point value. Similarly, the precision specified for int will be used as the default precision for all integer-based variables.

It is not mandatory to specify precision qualifiers for variables in vertex shaders, because they have a pre-defined default precision for int and float types. However, in fragment shaders, although (at least) medium precision is supported for float types, (unlike vertex shaders) it is not set as the default precision. This means that every fragment shader must explicitly declare a default precision for float types.

ES 2.0 allows us to determine the availability of high precision for the float type, and, if it is not available, we can fall back to medium precision by setting it as the default precision for all float types in a fragment shader. To determine whether high precision is supported in the fragment shader, we need to find out whether the GL_FRAGMENT_PRECISION_HIGH preprocessor macro is defined (as shown in Listing 3-14).

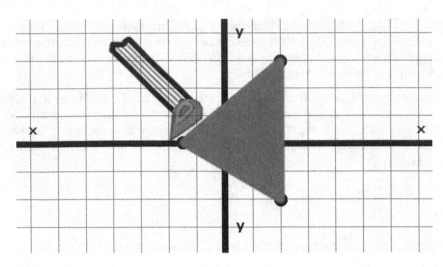

Figure 3-9. Fragment shading

GL POINT BASIC Application

Shader code (_pointVertexShaderCode, _pointFragmentShaderCode) inside the Renderer class (GL POINT BASIC/src/com/apress/android/glpointbasic/GLES20Renderer.java) must be compiled into a binary format so the GPU can process it. There are three ES 2.0 functions—glCreateShader, glShaderSource, and glCompileShader—that we have to use every time we compile a vertex and a fragment shader.

Once we have compiled the *shaders* for an object (recall that an object is a primitive or a combination of same type of primitives), we must create an ES 2.0 ***program*** for it (not to be confused with the *shader program*) that links the vertex and fragment shader as a unit. Using this ***program*** object, we render primitives on the OpenGL surface. To see these steps in action, import the archive file glpointbasic.zip from the *Chapter3* folder. This will load the *GL POINT BASIC* application into your Eclipse workspace.

Using the loadShader Method

The Renderer class contains the good old methods (onSurfaceCreated, onSurfaceChanged, and onDrawFrame), using which we can easily organize code for different purposes (which we previously discussed). There are two primary changes in this class—*shader programs* and the loadShader method—and, from this point forward, we use these in all ES 2.0 applications.

I already explained the use of *shaders* (to render a point sprite primitive, the Renderer class contains both vertex and fragment shaders), so let's talk about the loadShader method (Listing 3-15).

Listing 3-15. GL POINT BASIC/src/com/apress/android/glpointbasic/GLES20Renderer.java

```
private int loadShader(int type, String source)  {
 int shader = GLES20.glCreateShader(type);
 GLES20.glShaderSource(shader, source);
 GLES20.glCompileShader(shader);
 return shader;
}
```

Inside this method, there are three ES 2.0 functions to help us with the compilation of shaders. Using `int shader = GLES20.glCreateShader(type)`, shader-object is created for a specific type of *shader* (`GLES20.GL_VERTEX_SHADER` or `GLES20.GL_FRAGMENT_SHADER`). Then, the shader source code (vertex or fragment shader code) is loaded to this object using `glShaderSource` function, which is finally compiled using `glCompileShader` function and is then returned. Please note that shader source code of each type (that is, vertex and fragment shader) needs to be loaded to this shader-object before it can be used in an ES 2.0 *program*.

Inside the `onSurfaceCreated` or `onSurfaceChanged` method, we use these compiled shaders by creating an ES 2.0 *program* using the `glCreateProgram` function. Compiled shaders must be loaded to this *program* using `glAttachShader` before they are finally linked as a unit (Listing 3-16).

Listing 3-16. GL POINT BASIC/src/com/apress/android/glpointbasic/GLES20Renderer.java

```
int pointVertexShader = loadShader(GLES20.GL_VERTEX_SHADER, _pointVertexShaderCode);
int pointFragmentShader = loadShader(GLES20.GL_FRAGMENT_SHADER, _pointFragmentShaderCode);
_pointProgram = GLES20.glCreateProgram();
GLES20.glAttachShader(_pointProgram, pointVertexShader);
GLES20.glAttachShader(_pointProgram, pointFragmentShader);
GLES20.glLinkProgram(_pointProgram);
```

Attributes

Before we explain this application further, make few additions to the Renderer class. Include the fields `int _pointAVertexLocation` and `FloatBuffer _pointVFB` to this class. Then, create a new method `initShapes()` with type void. Inside this method, add the lines of code from Listing 3-17. Call `initShapes` anywhere inside `onSurfaceChanged` method.

Listing 3-17. GL POINT ADVANCED/src/com/apress/android/glpointadvanced/GLES20Renderer.java

```
float[] pointVFA = {
  0.1f,0.1f,0.0f,
  -0.1f,0.1f,0.0f,
  -0.1f,-0.1f,0.0f,
  0.1f,-0.1f,0.0f
};
ByteBuffer pointVBB = ByteBuffer.allocateDirect(pointVFA.length * 4);
pointVBB.order(ByteOrder.nativeOrder());
_pointVFB = pointVBB.asFloatBuffer();
_pointVFB.put(pointVFA);
_pointVFB.position(0);
```

Using this code, we create a `FloatBuffer` (`_pointVFB`) to represent four points in each quadrant shown in Figure 3-6. After making a few additional changes to this class, you can render these points on OpenGL surface (Figure 3-10).

Figure 3-10. GL POINT ADVANCED

Replace the vertex shader code with lines given in Listing 3-18. This code demonstrates that we can also supply inputs to vertex shaders "externally," instead of directly defining and writing data to gl_Position variable.

Listing 3-18. GL POINT ADVANCED/src/com/apress/android/glpointadvanced/GLES20Renderer.java

```
private final String _pointVertexShaderCode =
  "attribute vec4 aPosition;"
+ "void main() {"
+ " gl_PointSize = 15.0;"
+ " gl_Position = aPosition;"
+ "}";
```

To supply input data, we use *attribute* variables. Like gl_PointSize and gl_Position variables, attribute variables are only available in the vertex shader. They are used to specify the per-vertex inputs to the vertex shader (per-vertex inputs, such as position and color).

Using the glGetAttribLocation method, we first access the attribute variable inside the vertex shader of a ***program***. Only then can we pass data to it. For the Renderer class, field _pointAVertexLocation stores the location of the attribute variable aPosition using _pointAVertexLocation = GLES20.glGetAttribLocation(_pointProgram, "aPosition"). Add this line after ES 2.0 function glLinkProgram shown in Listing 3-16.

Finally, inside the onDrawFrame method, we use the FloatBuffer _pointVFB to pass per-vertex data (in this case, the per-vertex data is the vertex itself; that is, the coordinate representing the vertex) to the attribute variable aPosition. If we only want to render a single point sprite, there is no need to go through all these steps. We can directly write to the gl_Position variable as shown in Listing 3-8. To obtain output as shown in Figure 3-10, replace the onDrawFrame method with Listing 3-20.

To pass per-vertex data (such as per-vertex colors, per-vertex normals, or, as in this case, the coordinate representing this vertex) to the aPosition variable, we use the method glVertexAttribPointer(int indx, int size, int type, boolean normalized, int stride, Buffer ptr). Based on the type of per-vertex data we are dealing with, we specify the size of this data as int size. For example, if we are passing per-vertex position data (that is, vertex coordinate), for a single vertex (x, y, z) or a set of vertices (pointVFA in Listing 3-17), then size will be '3.' Similarly, if we are passing per-vertex colors (r, g, b, a), size will be '4.'

Listing 3-19. GL POINT ADVANCED/src/com/apress/android/glpointadvanced/GLES20Renderer.java

```
GLES20.glVertexAttribPointer(_pointAVertexLocation, 3, GLES20.GL_FLOAT, false, 12, _pointVFB);
GLES20.glEnableVertexAttribArray(_pointAVertexLocation);
```

For data containing floating-point values, the type argument is GLES20.GL_FLOAT. We must use this type for position, as well as for color data. We do not want to normalize the vertex data, so, we set the boolean argument to false. We use the stride argument if storing various types of per-vertex data inside the same float array. For all cases in which we store a single type of vertex data, such as vertex positions, inside a float array, we set stride as '0' or size * the size of type argument. The indx and ptr arguments are for attribute location and buffer (FloatBuffer _pointVFB), respectively. If you look closely at Listings 3-18 and 3-19, you will see that the attribute variable inside the vertex shader code is of type vec4, whereas the size argument in glVertexAttribPointer is '3.' Well, the vertex shader can understand what we are doing here; since we are rendering a vertex, it appends the extra component to make the rendering possible. After calling the function glVertexAttribPointer, we must also activate the corresponding attribute location, by calling glEnableVertexAttribArray, which takes the location of attribute variable as an argument.

> **Note**   While glVertexAttribPointer tells OpenGL about the format (and source) of our vertex array data, glEnableVertexAttribArray activates the given attribute location, so that, finally, OpenGL can pull this vertex data.

Listing 3-20. GL POINT ADVANCED/src/com/apress/android/glpointadvanced/GLES20Renderer.java

```
public void onDrawFrame(GL10 gl) {
 GLES20.glClear(GLES20.GL_COLOR_BUFFER_BIT | GLES20.GL_DEPTH_BUFFER_BIT);
 GLES20.glUseProgram(_pointProgram);
 GLES20.glVertexAttribPointer(_pointAVertexLocation, 3, GLES20.GL_FLOAT, false, 12, _pointVFB);
 GLES20.glEnableVertexAttribArray(_pointAVertexLocation);
 GLES20.glDrawArrays(GLES20.GL_POINTS, 0, 4);
}
```

The call to ES 2.0 functions—glVertexAttribPointer and glEnableVertexAttribArray (and others explained in the following section)—inside onDrawFrame is sandwiched between function calls for using an ES 2.0 **program** (glUseProgram in Listing 3-20) and drawing primitives (glDrawArrays or glDrawElements). This must be done every time we render an object (that is, a primitive or a combination of same type of primitives).

I'll deal with the glDrawElements function in Chapter 4. Here, I explain glDrawArrays. This method takes three arguments—mode, first, and count—all of type int. Using mode, we specify the type of primitive we want to render. We work with modes GL_POINTS, GL_LINES, and GL_TRIANGLES, but please be aware that ES 2.0 also provides alternate modes (GL_LINE_STRIP, GL_LINE_LOOP, GL_TRIANGLE_STRIP, and GL_TRIANGLE_FAN). GL_POINTS mode is very straightforward. By calling glDrawArrays(GLES20.GL_POINTS, 0, 4), we notify the vertex shader that we want to render four points (point sprites) on the OpenGL surface. The second argument is '0,' because we want to render from the first vertex inside pointVFA (0.1f, 0.1f, 0.0f) in Listing 3-17.

Similarly, for rendering a line primitive, we call glDrawArrays(GLES20.GL_LINES, 0, 2), and for a triangle primitive, we call glDrawArrays(GLES20.GL_TRIANGLES, 0, 3). Next, I'll show you how to render a line, triangle, and rectangle using glDrawArrays.

Drawing Line and Triangle Primitives

For the following applications, you may use the *GL POINT ADVANCED* application (glpointadvanced.zip) as a template. To render a line primitive (Figure 3-11) using glDrawArrays method, we must make sure we set its mode argument as GLES20.GL_LINES. Since a line requires two points, while rendering a line primitive, the count argument (the last argument in the glDrawArrays method) should be at least '2.'

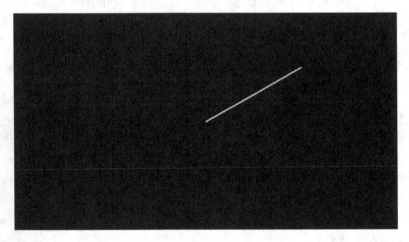

Figure 3-11. Line primitive

After appropriately setting the arguments for glDrawArrays, we must create an array to store the endpoints of line(s). So, inside the template you can modify the contents of the float array pointVFA (inside initShapes method), and, to get an output similar to Figure 3-11, define this array as {0.0f,0.0f,0.0f, 0.5f,0.5f,0.0f}. Since this array has two points, we must call glDrawArrays using glDrawArrays(GLES20.GL_LINES, 0, 2).

Before you run this application, remove the line "gl_PointSize = 15.0;" from the vertex shader. As previously stated, gl_PointSize variable is only used with a point sprite primitive. To set the width of line primitive, call the method GLES20.glLineWidth(float width) before calling GLES20.glDrawArrays. The default width is 1.0.

Varyings

Like vertex shaders, fragment shaders have a special kind of input variable, called *varying*. They are special, because they are used to store the output of the vertex shader, as well as the input of a fragment shader.

Varyings interpolate values across a primitive, and this becomes useful when creating cool gradients (as shown in Figure 3-12) or interpolating texture coordinates and normals (as we see in Chapter 5).

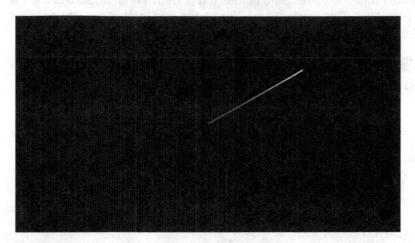

Figure 3-12. Using varying in vertex shaders

To use a varying variable, it should be declared in a vertex and fragment shader such that it has same type in both shaders. To understand this, import the archive file glvarying.zip from the *Chapter3* folder. This will load the *GL VARYING* application into your workspace. If you browse through the contents of the Renderer class, you will see right away that it is for rendering a line primitive.

First, notice the initShapes method inside the Renderer class. Apart from the float array for vertex positions (lineVFA), it contains another array—lineCFA. The first four elements in this array (0, 0, 1, 1) represent blue color, whereas the last four elements (1, 1, 0, 1) represent yellow color. This per-vertex color data is passed to the attribute variable aColor (recall that float array for an attribute is passed as FloatBuffer) using the ES 2.0 function glVertexAttribPointer, as shown in Listing 3-21.

Listing 3-21. GL VARYING/src/com/apress/android/glvarying/GLES20Renderer.java

```
public void onDrawFrame(GL10 gl) {
 GLES20.glClear(GLES20.GL_COLOR_BUFFER_BIT | GLES20.GL_DEPTH_BUFFER_BIT);
 GLES20.glUseProgram(_lineProgram);
 GLES20.glVertexAttribPointer(_lineAVertexLocation, 3, GLES20.GL_FLOAT, false, 0, _lineVFB);
 GLES20.glEnableVertexAttribArray(_lineAVertexLocation);
 GLES20.glVertexAttribPointer(_lineAColorLocation, 4, GLES20.GL_FLOAT, false, 0, _lineCFB);
 GLES20.glEnableVertexAttribArray(_lineAColorLocation);
 GLES20.glLineWidth(3);
 GLES20.glDrawArrays(GLES20.GL_LINES, 0, 2);
}
```

Next, take a look at the vertex and fragment shaders (Listing 3-22). Notice how the varying variable vColor is shared by each of these shaders. As previously mentioned, its type should match in both the shaders.

Inside the vertex shader, vColor receives per-vertex color data (blue and yellow color) from the attribute variable aColor. When the rendering pipeline processes the fragments using fragment shader, it interpolates this per-vertex data across the primitive (that is, across the fragments occupied by the primitive). This is why blue color at one endpoint of the line primitive interpolates to yellow color at the other (Figure 3-12).

Listing 3-22. GL VARYING/src/com/apress/android/glvarying/GLES20Renderer.java

```
private final String _lineVertexShaderCode =
   "attribute vec4 aPosition;"
 + "attribute vec4 aColor;"
 + "varying vec4 vColor;"
 + "void main() {"
 + " vColor = aColor;"
 + " gl_Position = aPosition;"
 + "}";

private final String _lineFragmentShaderCode =
   "#ifdef GL_FRAGMENT_PRECISION_HIGH \n"
 + "precision highp float;"
 + "#else \n"
 + "precision mediump float;"
 + "#endif \n"
 + "varying vec4 vColor;"
 + "void main() {"
 + " gl_FragColor = vColor;"
 + "}";
```

As explained in the section "GLSL", every fragment shader must explicitly declare a default precision for float types, such as vec4, which is why there is extra code at the top of fragment shader in Listing 3-22. (Refer back to that topic for more on the basics of data types.)

Triangle Primitive

Like a line primitive, rendering a triangle primitive (Figure 3-13) requires appropriately setting the arguments of the glDrawArrays function. We must specify the mode as GLES20.GL_TRIANGLES and the count as a multiple of 3 (you get an imaginary triangle if you set the count to 0!).

Figure 3-13. Rendering triangle using glDrawArrays

Rendering a triangle primitive is left as an exercise for you, but, in case you find this difficult, you can import the archive file gltriangle.zip from the source code for this chapter. This will load the *GL TRIANGLE* application into your Eclipse workspace.

As previously mentioned, in ES 2.0 we can use a combination of the same type of primitives to render various objects. Now, let's look at rendering a rectangle using two triangle primitives.

Using glDrawArrays, with mode GL_TRIANGLES, an easy way to render a rectangle is by creating a float array for points that form a closed loop. When we call glDrawArrays for such a collection of points, we need to pass the count argument as '6.' The float array given in Listing 3-23 is a collection of three points for each of the upper and lower triangles.

Listing 3-23. GL RECTANGLE/src/com/apress/android/glrectangle/GLES20Renderer.java

```
float rectangleVFA[] = {
    0, 0, 0,
    0, 0.5f, 0,
    0.75f, 0.5f, 0, // upper triangle
    0.75f, 0.5f, 0,
    0.75f, 0, 0,
    0, 0, 0, // lower triangle
};
```

You must make three changes to the *GL POINT ADVANCED* application to render a rectangle as shown in Figure 3-14:

1. Remove the line " gl_PointSize = 15.0; \n" from the point vertex shader code (_pointVertexShaderCode).

2. Replace the contents of array pointVFA (inside initShapes method) with the points given in Listing 3-23.

3. Modify the call to GLES20.glDrawArrays method as GLES20.glDrawArrays(GLES20.GL_TRIANGLES, 0, 6);.

Figure 3-14. Rendering rectangle using triangle primitives

Normalized Device Coordinate System

To simplify things, OpenGL ES assumes that the vertices specified for primitives (Listing 3-24) are for a 3D world, which is a normalized cube, so that all points in this cube lie within the range [1, 1, 1] to [-1, -1, -1]. To see this, import the archive file ndc.zip from the source code for this chapter.

Listing 3-24. NDC/src/com/apress/android/ndc/GLES20Renderer.java

```
float triangleVFA[] = {
    -1.0f, 0.0f, 0.0f,
    1.0f, 0.0f, 0.0f,
    0.0f, 1.0f, 0.0f
};
```

If you read the Renderer class of the *NDC* application, you will see that it is trying to render a triangle primitive. Inside the initShapes method, the float array (triangleVFA) for position is defined as shown in Listing 3-24.

When you run this application, you get output similar to Figures 3-15 and 3-16 (for portrait and landscape modes respectively). As mentioned, OpenGL ES assumes that the vertices specified for triangle primitive are for a normalized cube world. When graphics are rendered using OpenGL ES, this cube world is projected onto the (rectangular) 2D space of display screen, causing them to appear skewed (Figures 3-15 and 3-16).

Figure 3-15. *Normalized Device Coordinate System (portrait mode)*

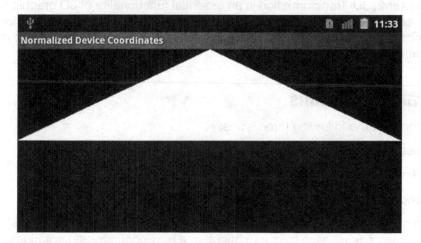

Figure 3-16. *Normalized Device Coordinate System (landscape mode)*

OpenGL ES renders an object (that is, a primitive or a combination of the same type of primitives) using a normalized coordinate system. Normalized Device Coordinate System (*NDCS*) is the coordinate system in which the entire screen of the device corresponds to a unit cube, so all points in this cube are within the range [1, 1, 1] to [-1, -1, -1] for x, y, and z, as shown in Figure 3-17.

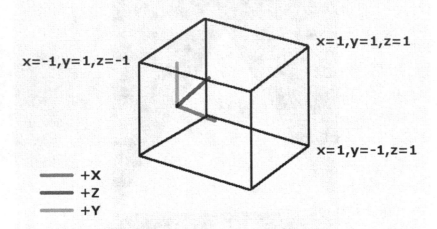

Figure 3-17. Normalized 3D space

Another important feature of this coordinate system is that it is *left handed*, meaning the point (0, 0, -1) in this coordinate system lies closer to the viewer than the point (0, 0, 1). Apart from *NDCS*, there are other coordinate systems in the vertex rendering stages of the graphics pipeline; however, we are more concerned with *NDCS*, because we can transform it to act like a real world. This is illustrated in the following section.

3D-Transformation

As shown in Chapter 2, 3D-Transformation is an essential functionality of 3D graphic rendering APIs, which we use to change sizes, orientations, or positions of objects by matrix operations. Now, I'll briefly explain each of the following transformations and describe the order in which these are used in ES 2.0 applications.

Types of Transformations

3D-Transformation is of the following three types:

- Geometric/Modeling transformation
- Coordinate/Viewing transformation
- Perspective/Projection transformation

Using geometric transformation, we can transform an object to a new position (translation transformation), a new size (scaling transformation), or a new configuration (rotation transformation). An important feature of this transformation is that it is applied only to the object and not the coordinate system in which it is placed.

Matrices for geometric transformations (*translate*, *rotate*, and *scale* matrices) require factors per-axis for the corresponding transformation. Therefore, to translate an object along the x-axis (Figure 3-18), say from (1, 0, 0) to (5, 0, 0), we need to update the *translate matrix* with the desired axis (x-axis) and the factor (four in this case).

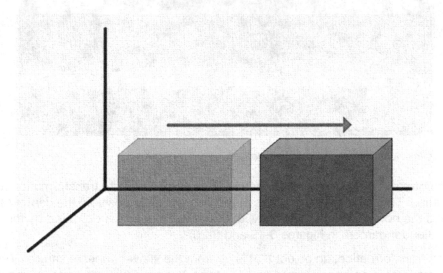

Figure 3-18. Translation along +X axis

Coordinate (or viewing) transformation is analogous to geometric transformation, but there is a striking difference between the two. Instead of affecting an object, coordinate transformation affects the viewer (Figures 3-19 and 3-20) to produce results similar to geometric transformation.

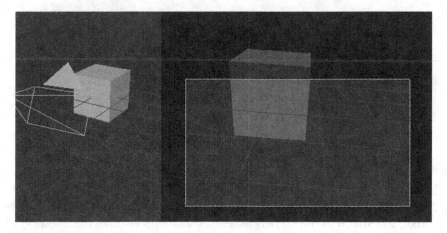

Figure 3-19. Viewing transformation

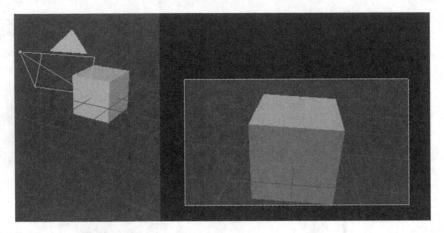

Figure 3-20. Viewing transformation, changing viewer's position

Geometric transformation requires per-axis factors, whereas coordinate transformation requires viewing information. This information consists of the viewer's (eye) position, the center of observation, and the normal ("vector" quantity) to the viewer's head (as indicated by the orange arrow over the Blender camera in Figures 3-19 and 3-20).

Using projection transformation, an object that is far from the viewer appears smaller. This transformation provides a perspective into the 3D scene using a viewing volume, as indicated by the (blue) frustum in Figure 3-21.

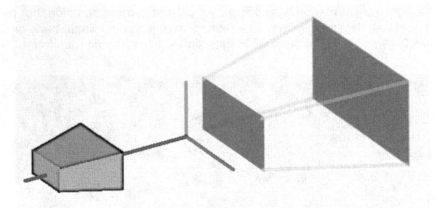

Figure 3-21. Viewing volume

Projection transformation allows control of the projection of cube world of *NDCS* (Figure 3-17) onto the (rectangular) 2D space of the display screen. This helps remove the skewing of rendered graphics (since we limit the viewing volume, graphics no longer stretch when the orientation changes). Additionally, the final coordinate system becomes *right handed* (that is, point (0, 0, 1) in this coordinate system is closer to the viewer than point (0, 0, -1)).

The Matrix Class

Most graphic rendering APIs do not provide built-in functions for transformations. However, frameworks hosting such APIs do provide utility methods for the same. Once again, Android comes to the rescue, providing useful methods for transformations using the `android.opengl.Matrix` class (not to be confused with the `android.graphics.Matrix` class). The following is a list of matrix math utilities from this class to help easily perform the transformations discussed so far:

Geometric/Modeling transformation

- `Matrix.`*`translateM(float[] m, int mOffset, float x, float y, float z):`*
  Translates matrix m by x, y, and z along x-axis, y-axis, and z-axis, respectively
  (please note that, for all methods we use from the `Matrix` class, we set the
  `mOffset` argument as '0,' which means "no-offset")

- `Matrix.`*`rotateM(float[] m, int mOffset, float a, float x, float y, float z):`*
  Rotates matrix m by angle a (in degrees) about the specified axes

- `Matrix.`*`scaleM(float[] m, int mOffset, float x, float y, float z):`* Scales
  matrix m by x, y, and z along x-axis, y-axis, and z-axis, respectively

Coordinate/Viewing transformation

- `Matrix.`*`setLookAtM(float[] m, int mOffset, float eyeX, float eyeY, float
  eyeZ, float centerX, float centerY, float centerZ, float upX, float upY,
  float upZ):`* Defines a *view matrix* m in terms of an eye point (that is, viewer's
  position), a center of view, and an up vector.

Perspective/Projection transformation

- `Matrix.`*`frustumM(float[] m, int mOffset, float left, float right, float
  bottom, float top, float near, float far):`* Defines a *projection matrix* m in
  terms of six clip planes

To perform these transformations, we need to associate matrices with objects (again, an object is a primitive or a combination of same type of primitives). There are three stages—first, we declare a new kind of input variable in our vertex shader called *uniform*; then we multiply this variable with an *attribute* so as to transform per-vertex position data; finally, we "externally" pass data to this *uniform* variable. You may have guessed that this data consists of Java `float` arrays.

We describe this with the help of an application, but first we explain an important concept about combined transformations. In almost all cases, when working with transformations of objects in interactive ES 2.0 applications, we have to use modeling transformation in combination with viewing and projection transformations. We can use a single matrix to represent all of these transformations, and we usually call this as **MVPmatrix** (that is, *Model-View-Projection matrix*). It bears this name to signify the order in which we combine the transformations so they are represented as a single matrix. We first update the **MVPmatrix** with any of the modeling transformations, say using the `translateM` method. Then, we update it with the `setLookAtM` method to apply viewing transformation. Finally, using the `frustumM` method, we apply projection transformation. Please note that, because of the way matrices work, this order (that is, *Model-View-Projection*) becomes important when combining transformations.

From the source code for this chapter, import the archive file glcube.zip. This loads the *GL CUBE* application into your workspace. First, turn your attention to the onSurfaceChanged method of the Renderer class.

setLookAtM method (Listing 3-25) defines a *view matrix* _ViewMatrix (fields named as _*Matrix are float arrays of size 16) in terms of an eye point (-13, 5, 10), a center of view (0, 0, 0), and an up vector (0, 1, 0) for (x, y, z).

Listing 3-25. GL CUBE/src/com/apress/android/glcube/GLES20Renderer.java

```
float ratio = (float) width / height;
float zNear = 0.1f;
float zFar = 1000;
float fov = 0.75f; // 0.2 to 1.0
float size = (float) (zNear * Math.tan(fov / 2));
Matrix.setLookAtM(_ViewMatrix, 0, -13, 5, 10, 0, 0, 0, 0, 1, 0);
Matrix.frustumM(_ProjectionMatrix, 0, -size, size, -size / ratio, size / ratio, zNear, zFar);
Matrix.multiplyMM(_MVPMatrix, 0, _ProjectionMatrix, 0, _ViewMatrix, 0);
```

In Listing 3-25, the code snippet used above the setLookAtM method (that is, the lines of code from "float ratio = (float) width/height" to "float size = (float) (zNear * Math.tan(fov / 2))") is used to prepare the arguments for the frustumM method. This method defines the viewing volume in terms of left-right, bottom-top, and near-far planes. Finally, using another utility method multiplyMM from the android.opengl.Matrix class, the result of _ProjectionMatrix * _ViewMatrix is stored in _MVPMatrix.

In the *GL CUBE* application, if any modeling transformation was used (for example, rotation), the last line in Listing 3-25 would look similar to Listing 3-26 (Chapter4/gltankfenceelements1.zip). Effectively, this would store the result of _ProjectionMatrix * _ViewMatrix * _RMatrix in _MVPMatrix. Here (Listing 3-26), the _RMatrix stores the modeling transformation of type rotation.

Listing 3-26. TANK FENCE ELEMENTS 1/src/com/apress/android/tankfenceelements1/GLES20Renderer.java

```
Matrix.multiplyMM(_MVPMatrix, 0, _ViewMatrix, 0, _RMatrix, 0);
Matrix.multiplyMM(_MVPMatrix, 0, _ProjectionMatrix, 0, _MVPMatrix, 0);
```

Inside the vertex shader (Listing 3-27), a uniform variable is declared (similar to the way we declare an attribute). Uniforms are variables that store read only values. They are generally used to store values, such as transformation matrices, that need to be updated "externally." They are read only within the vertex shader; however, if any geometric transformation needs performed on a frame by frame basis, we can pass data to uniform variables at run time using the ES 2.0 function GLES20.glUniformMatrix4fv.

Listing 3-27. GL CUBE/src/com/apress/android/glcube/GLES20Renderer.java

```
private final String _cubeVertexShaderCode =
  "attribute vec3 aPosition;"
+ "attribute vec4 aColor;"
+ "varying vec4 vColor;"
+ "uniform mat4 uMVP;"
+ "void main() {"
```

```
+ " vColor = aColor;"
+ " vec4 vertex = vec4(aPosition[0],aPosition[1],aPosition[2],1.0);"
+ " gl_Position = uMVP * vertex;"
+ "}";
```

Variable gl_Position is finally assigned the value uMVP * vertex. In this multiplication, the matrix comes before per-vertex position data, because matrices in OpenGL ES (mat2, mat3, and mat4) are stored in column major order (the methods of Matrix class also operate on column-vector matrices because of this). Please note that, if vertex variable inside main was of type vec3, the result of multiplication would have been invalid, as the uniform variable uMVP is of type mat4 (recall, that mat4 is a square matrix).

Like glGetAttribLocation, glGetUniformLocation is used to obtain the location of uniform variable. Renderer class has field _cubeUMVPLocation to store this location, and location of uniform is stored using _cubeUMVPLocation = GLES20.glGetUniformLocation(_cubeProgram, "uMVP");.

Finally, this value is loaded to the uniform variable by calling GLES20.glUniformMatrix4fv(_cubeUMVPLocation, 1, false, _MVPMatrix, 0). As shown in Figure 3-22, the rendered cube is incomplete. It is an exercise for you to complete this cube.

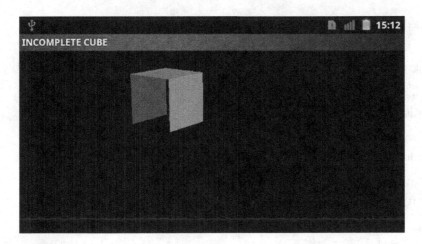

Figure 3-22. GL CUBE application

State Management

As you already know, there are various stages in the ES 2.0 rendering pipeline. These stages have states that can be enabled or disabled. Here, we examine two important stages in the rendering pipeline.

Cull Face

When we render triangle primitives, the rendering pipeline allows us to specify which triangles are back-facing and which are front-facing. This is not by virtue of face pointing viewer, but is based on the following orientations of the (vertices of) triangle—Clockwise (CW) and Counter-Clockwise

(CCW). Then, using state GL_CULL_FACE, we can cull (discard) triangles that are back-facing or front-facing.

> **Note** With the help of culling, our application does not send draw commands for discarded objects. This is useful, as it can improve the rendering performance.

To understand this, import the archive file Chapter3/glcullface.zip. This loads the *GL CULL FACE* application into your workspace (this application is almost identical to the *GL CUBE* application). If you turn your attention to the per-vertex position data (Listing 3-28) specified in cubeVFA, you observe that it contains vertices for six triangles (for an output similar to Figure 3-22)—two triangles each for back/front side and two for the top side of the incomplete cube shown in Figure 3-22.

Listing 3-28. GL CULL FACE/src/com/apress/android/glcullface/GLES20Renderer.java

```
float[] cubeVFA = {
  0,0,-4,
  0,2,-4,
  2,2,-4, // back half
  2,2,-4,
  2,0,-4,
  0,0,-4, // back half
  2,2,-4,
  0,2,-4,
  0,2,-2, // top half
  0,2,-2,
  2,2,-2,
  2,2,-4, // top half
  2,2,-2,
  0,2,-2,
  0,0,-2, // front half
  0,0,-2,
  2,0,-2,
  2,2,-2, // front half
};
```

Vertices for each of the triangles on the back side are arranged in a CW orientation, whereas others are arranged in a CCW orientation. This is done intentionally to discard triangles that have CW orientation (that is, a triangle whose vertices are arranged in a CW manner). To make the rendering pipeline aware of the culling state, we proceed as shown in Listing 3-29.

Listing 3-29. GL CULL FACE/src/com/apress/android/glcullface/GLES20Renderer.java

```
GLES20.glEnable(GLES20.GL_CULL_FACE);
GLES20.glCullFace(GLES20.GL_BACK);
GLES20.glFrontFace(GLES20.GL_CCW);
```

First we enable the state GL_CULL_FACE. Then, using the ES 2.0 function glCullFace, we specify which face has to be culled—GL_FRONT or GL_BACK (GL_BACK is the default). Finally, using glFrontFace, we specify the orientation to be made front-facing. As a result, we get the output as shown in Figure 3-23 (instead of the output shown in Figure 3-22).

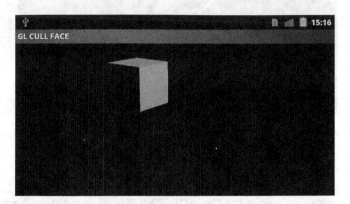

Figure 3-23. GL CULL FACE application

Depth Test

Apart from the color buffer, there is another kind of framebuffer associated with the *EGL* window— depth buffer. It is used for hidden surface removal. For each pixel on the OpenGL surface, it tracks (object) vertex's distance to the viewer to determine whether the corresponding fragment's color is retained on the color buffer. Therefore, if vertex B is behind vertex F, depth buffer stores the position of F (to further compare with other vertices for that pixel, if any) and stores its fragment corresponding to the matching pixel in color buffer.

An interesting point is that, when we only use a single ES 2.0 *program* in our Renderer class, "depth testing" takes place automatically. However, if there are multiple programs, we need to explicitly enable depth testing by calling "GLES20.glEnable(GLES20.GL_DEPTH_TEST)". If we do not enable it, the object rendered by the last *program* is considered to lie above other objects (that is, closer to the viewer) rendered using previous programs.

Another interesting point is that depth testing may seem to give unexpected results in *NDCS*, because *NDCS* has a *left handed* coordinate system. This can be corrected by adding the line "GLES20.glDepthRangef(1, 0);" after enabling GL_DEPTH_TEST; doing so changes *NDCS* into a *right handed* coordinate system. As discussed in the previous topic, we can also do this by using an *MVPmatrix* to transform per-vertex positions. To understand this more clearly, go through the Renderer class (GLES20Renderer) inside the *GL DEPTH TEST* application (Chapter3/gldepthtest.zip). Each of the *programs* used in this class renders a line primitive (Figure 3-24) and uses an *MVPmatrix* to transform per-vertex positions.

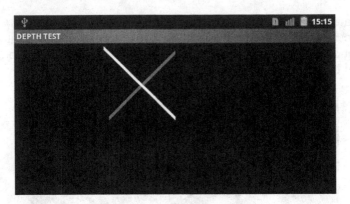

Figure 3-24. GL DEPTH TEST application

Summary

In this chapter you learned more about the OpenGL ES 2.0 environment on Android by examining:

- *EGL,* the software that helps us connect OpenGL ES 2.0 API with Android
- *GLSurfaceView class,* to manage the *EGL* window i.e. rendering surface
- *renderer thread,* which renders 3D graphics on the *EGL* window

After learning about the relationship between UI/main thread and renderer thread, you saw some applications that helped you understand the fundamental concepts of the OpenGL ES 2.0 API. You learned to draw primitive shapes in ES 2.0, such as points, lines, and triangles, and added to your knowledge of transformations that help us take control of the view settings of 3D graphics.

In the next chapter, we will work with Blender to model 3D objects for the *Tank Fence* game, and then I shall explain the use of parsers to integrate these objects easily into our ES 2.0 applications.

Chapter 4

3D Modeling

In this chapter you will be introduced to modeling 3D objects using the open-source software Blender. First, you will learn the basics of the Blender interface, and how to model the objects for our *Tank Fence* game. Finally, you will see how we include these objects inside ES 2.0 applications by using parsers to read and manipulate the mesh data.

Drawing Shapes Using glDrawElements

To specify the type of primitive(s) we intend to render on the OpenGL surface, we use ES 2.0 functions—glDrawArrays or glDrawElements.

In Chapter 3 you learned about the ES 2.0 function glDrawArrays. This function is generally not used for rendering primitives in ES 2.0 applications, such as games. This is because, when authoring game objects in 3D-modeling software, the objects can have plenty of meshes that share vertices leading to redundant data in float arrays for vertex positions (Listing 4-1) and, consequently, redundant data in vertex buffers (FloatBuffer) created using these arrays. Chapter 3 provided an example (Chapter3/glrectangle.zip) with redundant vertex data.

Listing 4-1. GL RECTANGLE/src/com/apress/android/glrectangle/GLES20Renderer.java

```
float rectangleVFA[]={
    0, 0, 0,
    0, 0.5f, 0,
    0.75f, 0.5f, 0,
    0.75f, 0.5f, 0, // duplication
    0.75f, 0, 0,
    0, 0, 0,          // duplication
};
```

To avoid this redundancy, use glDrawElements and provide a float array consisting of unique vertices of the object, as well as another (short) array consisting of element indices to access vertices (from the float array) representing primitive(s).

> **Note**   Meshes are primary shapes, such as triangles, used to represent real world objects in modeling softwares similar to Blender. The following section, "Blender for Modeling," discusses them.

GL POINT ELEMENTS Application

Without modifying the output of the *GL POINT ADVANCED* application, as shown in Figure 3-10 (Chapter3/glpointadvanced.zip), you can replace the call to glDrawArrays with glDrawElements. Please note that the *shader* code remains the same. In the Renderer class of the *GL POINT ADVANCED* application, turn your attention to the initShapes method. Much as we create a FloatBuffer for the vertex array (Listing 4-2), we create a ShortBuffer for the index array (Listing 4-3).

Listing 4-2. GL POINT ADVANCED/src/com/apress/android/glpointadvanced/GLES20Renderer.java

```
private void initShapes() {
 float[] pointVFA={
   0.1f,0.1f,0.0f,   // first quadrant
   -0.1f,0.1f,0.0f,  // second quadrant
   -0.1f,-0.1f,0.0f, // third quadrant
   0.1f,-0.1f,0.0f   // fourth quadrant
 };
 ByteBuffer pointVBB=ByteBuffer.allocateDirect(pointVFA.length * 4);
 pointVBB.order(ByteOrder.nativeOrder());
 _pointVFB=pointVBB.asFloatBuffer();
 _pointVFB.put(pointVFA);
 _pointVFB.position(0);
}
```

Listing 4-3. GL POINT ELEMENTS/src/com/apress/android/glpointelements/GLES20Renderer.java

```
private void initShapes()  {
 float[] pointVFA={ // vertex (float) array
   0.1f,0.1f,0.0f,   // 0
   -0.1f,0.1f,0.0f,  // 1
   -0.1f,-0.1f,0.0f, // 2
   0.1f,-0.1f,0.0f   // 3
 };
 ByteBuffer pointVBB=ByteBuffer.allocateDirect(pointVFA.length * 4);
 pointVBB.order(ByteOrder.nativeOrder());
 _pointVFB=pointVBB.asFloatBuffer();
 _pointVFB.put(pointVFA);
 _pointVFB.position(0);

 short[] pointISA={ // index (short) array
   0,1,2,3
 };
```

```
ByteBuffer pointIBB=ByteBuffer.allocateDirect(pointISA.length * 2);
pointIBB.order(ByteOrder.nativeOrder());
_pointISB=pointIBB.asShortBuffer();
_pointISB.put(pointISA);
_pointISB.position(0);
}
```

After setting the position of the FloatBuffer using _pointVFB.position(0), create a short array to store (zero-based) index positions of the vertices in array pointVFA, as shown in Listing 4-3. If you want to render all the vertices from this vertex array, store all the indices {0, 1, 2, 3} in the short array (say pointISA). Then, store this index array in a ShortBuffer, as shown in Listing 4-3. Here, _pointISB is a field (that is, a member variable) of type ShortBuffer.

Finally, in the onDrawFrame method, remove the call to glDrawArrays, and replace it with the line of code in Listing 4-4.

Listing 4-4. GL POINT ELEMENTS/src/com/apress/android/glpointelements/GLES20Renderer.java

```
GLES20.glDrawElements(GLES20.GL_POINTS, 4, GLES20.GL_UNSIGNED_SHORT, _pointISB);
```

glDrawElements takes four arguments. The first argument is the mode (for the type of primitive), the second argument is the count of indices stored in the index array (if in place of '4' you specify '3', the point sprite in the fourth quadrant won't be rendered), the third argument is data type of index array, and the last argument is the index array buffer or the address of index array (Chapter 5 discusses the address argument). In Listing 4-4, the arguments are GL_POINTS, 4, GL_UNSIGNED_SHORT, and ShortBuffer _pointISB, respectively.

To see the Renderer class with all of these changes, import the archive file Chapter4/glpointelements.zip. This loads the *GL POINT ELEMENTS* application into your workspace. Please note that the *shader* _pointFragmentShaderCode still works if you remove the precision settings outside the main function.

Drawing Line and Triangle Primitives

Here, I describe how to create a wireframe rectangle, as shown in Figure 4-1, with the help of line primitives and glDrawElements. Import the archive file Chapter3/glline.zip into your workspace, and start making changes to the Renderer class in the loaded application *GL LINE*.

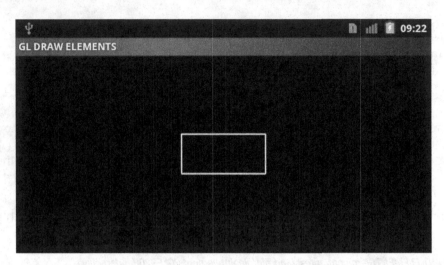

Figure 4-1. Rendering line primitives

Inside the initShapes method, initialize the vertex array lineVFA with vertices (four unique vertices) representing a rectangle. After storing this vertex array as a FloatBuffer, create the index array to access the vertices in lineVFA. Each line primitive requires two vertices; so, to create a wireframe rectangle from line primitives, use four sets of two vertices. Depending on the vertices you used inside lineVFA, you can create the index array containing eight indices, as shown in Listing 4-5. _lineISB is the buffer to store index array as a ShortBuffer. It is declared as a member variable.

Listing 4-5. GL LINE ELEMENTS/src/com/apress/android/gllineelements/GLES20Renderer.java

```
private void initShapes()  {
 float lineVFA[]={0.2f,0.2f,0.0f, -0.2f,0.2f,0.0f, -0.2f,-0.2f,0.0f, 0.2f,-0.2f,0.0f};
 ByteBuffer lineVBB=ByteBuffer.allocateDirect(lineVFA.length * 4);
 lineVBB.order(ByteOrder.nativeOrder());
 _lineVFB=lineVBB.asFloatBuffer();
 _lineVFB.put(lineVFA);
 _lineVFB.position(0);

 short lineISA[]={0,1, 1,2, 2,3, 3,0}; // 1,2 & 3 duplicated
 ByteBuffer lineIBB=ByteBuffer.allocateDirect(lineISA.length * 2);
 lineIBB.order(ByteOrder.nativeOrder());
 _lineISB=lineIBB.asShortBuffer();
 _lineISB.put(lineISA);
 _lineISB.position(0);
}
```

Finally, to render this wireframe rectangle, replace the call to glDrawArrays with glDrawElements using suitable arguments.

As shown in Listing 4-6, the mode argument is GL_LINES, the count argument is '8', the type argument is GL_UNSIGNED_SHORT, and the last argument is the ShortBuffer.

Listing 4-6. GL LINE ELEMENTS/src/com/apress/android/gllineelements/GLES20Renderer.java

```
GLES20.glDrawElements(GLES20.GL_LINES, 8, GLES20.GL_UNSIGNED_SHORT, _lineISB);
```

Rendering triangle primitives is left as an exercise for you; however, if you have any confusion about this, go through the Renderer class inside the *GL TRIANGLE ELEMENTS* application (Chapter4/gltriangleelements.zip). If you run this application, you see output similar to Figure 4-2.

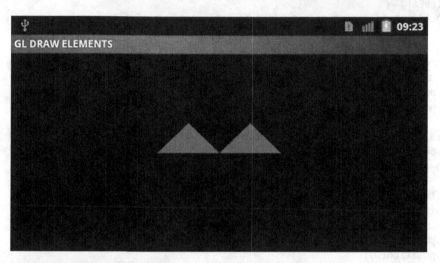

Figure 4-2. Triangle primitives using glDrawElements

Now, I describe how to create a rectangle (Figure 4-3) with the help of triangle primitives using glDrawElements. Once again, start by modifying the Renderer class inside the *GL RECTANGLE* application (Chapter3/glrectangle.zip).

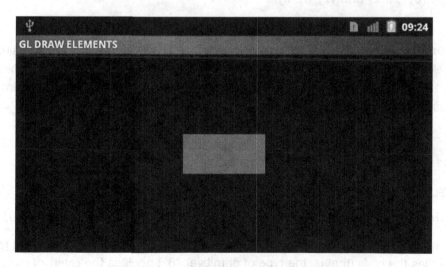

Figure 4-3. Rendering a rectangle using triangles

Inside the initShapes method, remove the duplicate vertices from the vertex array rectangleVFA shown in Listing 4-1. The array rectangleVFA is modified in Listing 4-7 to define a rectangle with different vertices. To render a rectangle using glDrawElements, this array must contain unique vertices corresponding to the corners of a rectangle.

Listing 4-7. GL RECTANGLE ELEMENTS/src/com/apress/android/glrectangleelements/GLES20Renderer.java

```
float rectangleVFA[]={
   0.2f,0.2f,0.0f, -0.2f,0.2f,0.0f, -0.2f,-0.2f,0.0f, 0.2f,-0.2f,0.0f
   };
ByteBuffer rectangleVBB=ByteBuffer.allocateDirect(rectangleVFA.length * 4);
rectangleVBB.order(ByteOrder.nativeOrder());
_rectangleVFB=rectangleVBB.asFloatBuffer();
_rectangleVFB.put(rectangleVFA);
_rectangleVFB.position(0);

short rectangleISA[]={
  0,1,2, // upper triangle
  2,3,0  // lower triangle
 };
ByteBuffer rectangleIBB=ByteBuffer.allocateDirect(rectangleISA.length * 2);
rectangleIBB.order(ByteOrder.nativeOrder());
_rectangleISB=rectangleIBB.asShortBuffer();
_rectangleISB.put(rectangleISA);
_rectangleISB.position(0);
```

Now, create the index array with sets of indices corresponding to upper and lower triangles (short[] rectangleISA, Listing 4-7). For example, if you used vertices {A, B, C, D} in the first, second, third, and fourth quadrants, respectively, to represent rectangle, then, one of the possible combinations of indices that can be used for rendering rectangle using glDrawElements with mode GL_TRIANGLES is {0, 1, 2} and {2, 3, 0}.

> **Note** glDrawElements draws a sequence of primitives using a vertex array and an additional (index) array with element indices for this vertex array. This function helps remove redundant data from the vertex array, and, as Chapter 5 shows, OpenGL ES may even cache recently processed vertices/indices and reuse them without resending them to the rendering pipeline.

Finally, replace the call to glDrawArrays with the line of code in Listing 4-8.

Listing 4-8. GL RECTANGLE ELEMENTS/src/com/apress/android/glrectangleelements/GLES20Renderer.java

```
GLES20.glDrawElements(GLES20.GL_TRIANGLES, 6, GLES20.GL_UNSIGNED_SHORT, _rectangleISB);
```

In Listing 4-8, the arguments passed to glDrawElements are straightforward. The GL_TRIANGLES argument specifies the mode (that is, the type of primitive), '6' specifies the count of indices in the index array, GL_UNSIGNED_SHORT specifies the data type of the index array, and the last argument specifies this index array as a `ShortBuffer`. Please note that, in the output, as shown in Figure 4-3, the rectangle is blue in color, as the fragment color is explicitly set to blue—`gl_FragColor=vec4(0,0,1,1);`

Now that you have a basic understanding of `glDrawElements`, you can start learning about 3D-content authoring software—in this case, Blender. Using Blender, we model 2D/3D objects, which can be parsed for vertex and index arrays for use with `glDrawElements`.

Blender for Modeling

Blender is a powerful 3D application for modeling, animation, rendering, compositing, video editing, and game creation. It is an open-source application and is available for the following OSes:

- Linux
- Mac OS X
- Windows
- FreeBSD

You can download Blender from the website `www.blender.org`. As it supports a wide range of OSes, you should take care to get the appropriate version for your OS.

> **Note**   Blender works the same on Windows and Mac OS X, but the keyboard on Mac does not have an *Alt* key.
> So, for all Blender examples demonstrated, replace the *Alt* key with the *Option* key, if you are using Mac.

Before moving ahead, when you start Blender, be sure to load its factory settings by selecting the option "Load Factory Settings" under the File menu, as shown in Figure 4-4.

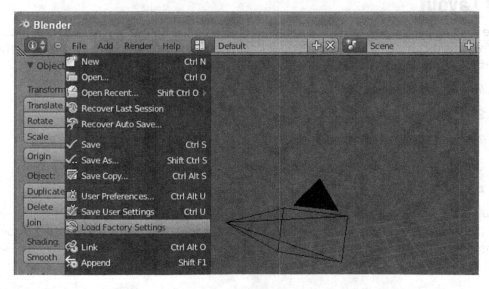

Figure 4-4. Loading the factory settings

Blender has a number of modes for working with objects (Figure 4-5).Here, we look at:

- *Object* Mode

- *Edit* Mode

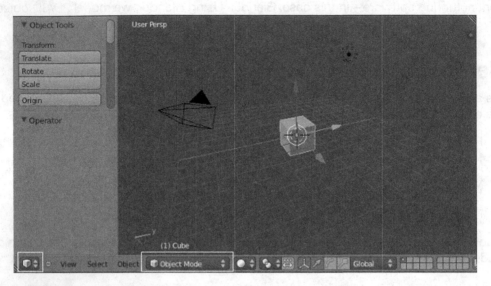

Figure 4-5. 3D View Window in Object Mode

Note   To toggle between these modes, hit the *Tab* key.

Default Layout

If you have loaded the factory settings and have not altered the default layout, you see the following five basic components in the Blender interface. These components are called windows. (Figures 4-54 to 4-57 at the end of this chapter show screen shots of the windows.)

1. *Info* Window : at the top

2. 3D Window a.k.a. *3D View* : at the center

3. *Timeline* Window : at the bottom

4. *Outliner* Window : at the upper-right corner

5. *Properties* Window : at the lower-right corner

All windows in Blender have a header, although in some cases the header may be located at the bottom of the window. Figure 4-5 shows the *3D View* (window), with its header at the bottom (for options—View, Select, Object, etc.). Please note that the entire layout shown in Figure 4-5 represents the *3D View*.

The *Info* window (see Figures 4-4 and 4-19) consists of useful menus (for example, File, Add, and Help), and it is only composed of a header.

> **Note**   You do not have to worry about the *Timeline* window; it is used for animations.

The *Outliner* window (the right half of Figures 4-7 and 4-8) lists all the objects added to the world-space of the *3D View*. *Outliner* window is used for selecting, deleting (Figure 4-17), and hiding objects modeled in Blender.

The *Properties* window (Figure 4-6) displays panels of functions. A panel is a set of related functions (for example, all of the rendering options are grouped under a panel "Render"). The header of the *Properties* window is a row of buttons—called *Context* buttons—that allow you to select which groups of panels are shown.

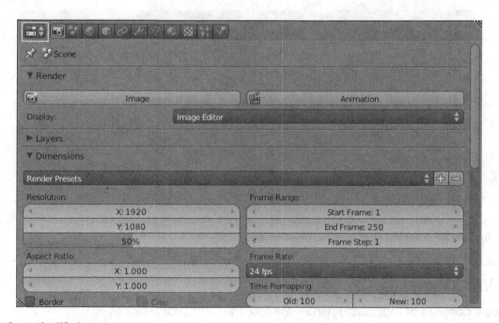

Figure 4-6. Properties Window

Most panels can be collapsed or expanded by clicking the solid black triangle, positioned left of the panel label, as shown in Figure 4-6. Similar to the *Properties* window, the *3D View* also consists of panels. In the following sections, we discuss these panels further.

Using Object Mode

The default mode in Blender is the *Object* mode. We usually work in this mode to translate, rotate, or scale object(s) added to the world-space of the *3D View*.

By default, the world-space loads with a cube at the center of the grid surface—the floor on which objects are placed. In addition, a camera and a lamp are also positioned somewhere close to the grid surface. The lamp aids the visibility of the object(s) when we render the world-space (as viewed from the camera) using the *F12* key. This is a shortcut key for the "Render Image" command in Blender.

> **Note**   Do not modify the positions of the lamp and camera. If you accidentally did, simply restart Blender.

To quickly select an object in the world-space, from the *Outliner* window, click the corresponding object label (for example, label "Cube"), as shown in Figure 4-7. You can toggle the visibility of an object in the world-space by clicking the "eye" image-button, corresponding to the object. Similarly, you can toggle the visibility of an object in the rendered image (*F12*) by clicking on the "camera" image-button, shown in Figure 4-7.

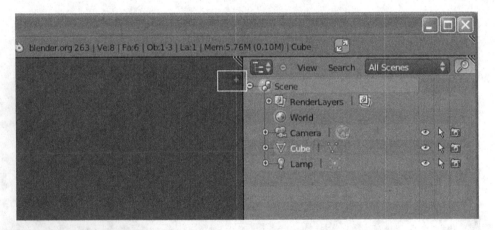

Figure 4-7. Toggling the properties shelf in the 3D View Window

Panels in 3D View

The *3D View* consists of toggleable parts—the *tool shelf* and *properties shelf*.

The *tool shelf* (Figure 4-5) consists of a useful panel, "Object-Tools." In this panel, you see buttons to translate, rotate, and scale object(s).

You can expand the *properties shelf* by clicking the small "plus" button at the top-right corner of the *3D View*. This button is highlighted within white border in Figure 4-7. Figure 4-8 shows the expanded *properties shelf*.

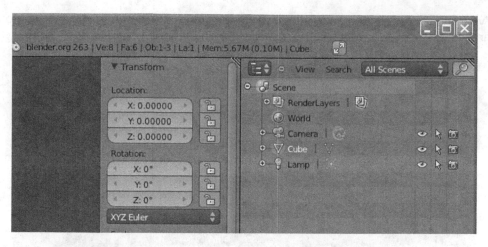

Figure 4-8. Properties shelf in 3D View Window

Unlike the functions in *tool shelf* ➤ *Object-Tools* panel, we explicitly provide (object) transformation values in functions listed under the *properties shelf* ➤ *Transform panel*.

> **Note** Do not confuse the *properties shelf* (Figures 4-7 and 4-8) with the *Properties* window (Figure 4-6).

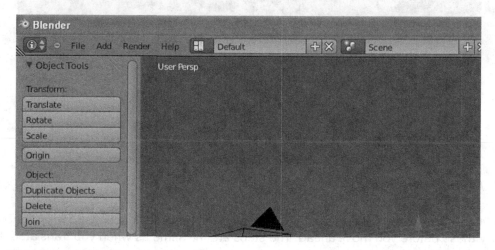

Figure 4-9. Object-Tools panel in the tool shelf

Translating Objects

Now, you will see how to translate objects along an axis. Select the cube object in the world-space by clicking the label "Cube" in the *Outliner* window. From the "Object-Tools" panel, click the "Translate" button under the label "Transform."

Once you've done this, press the *X* key. The cube in the world-space can now translate along a particular axis (Figure 4-10), which is the global x-axis in the world-space (of *3D View*).

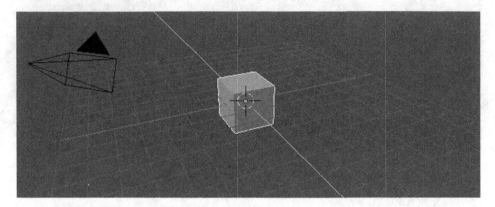

Figure 4-10. *Enabling constrained translation*

In Blender, translation of objects along a particular axis is called constrained translation. Just as you translated a cube along the global x-axis (Figure 4-11), you can also translate it along the y-axis and z-axis by pressing the *Y* and *Z* keys, respectively, after clicking the "Translate" button.

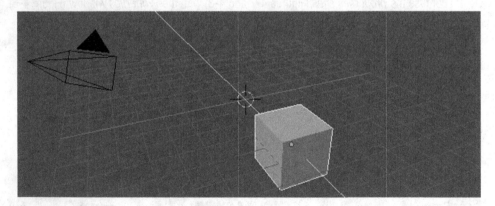

Figure 4-11. *Translating cube along global X axis*

As you have previously seen, the "Object-Tools" panel also provides functions to rotate and scale objects. Try these before you move ahead. The steps are the same as when you translated the cube.

Using the Lasso-Select Command

Now, I will show you how you can easily select multiple objects for various types of transformations. First, open the lassoSelect.blend file from the source code for this chapter (Blender/lassoSelect.blend) by double-clicking it.

The lassoSelect Blender file loads with three cubes in the world-space, as shown in Figure 4-12. Cubes can be added using the Add menu from the *Info* window.

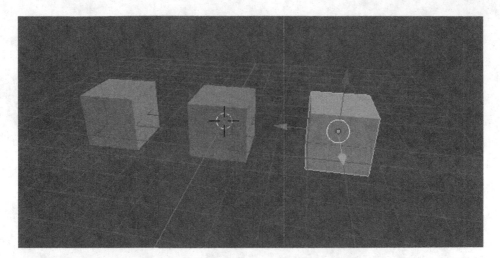

Figure 4-12. Default scene: lassoSelect Blender file

To select multiple objects using the lasso-select command, press *Ctrl* and then left-click and drag to enable the lasso. Now, without releasing the left-mouse-button (or left-touchpad-button), drag the lasso around the objects to completely encompass them (Figure 4-13).

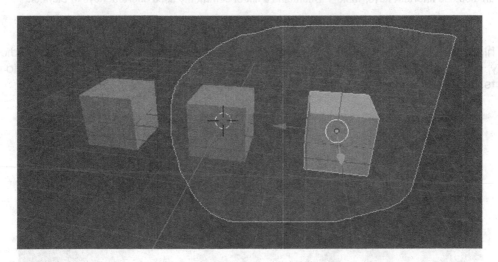

Figure 4-13. Selecting multiple objects

After completely surrounding the desired objects, release the left-mouse-button (or left-touchpad-button). This highlights the (lasso) selected objects (as shown in Figure 4-14), using which we can easily transform multiple objects.

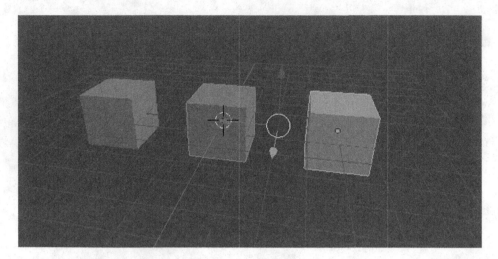

Figure 4-14. Highlighted objects

> **Note**   In place of transforming objects using buttons, listed under the "Object-Tools" panel (Figure 4-9), you can also use shortcut keys. Table 4-1 contains a list of commonly used shortcut keys in Blender.

To rotate highlighted objects (Figure 4-15), press the *R* key to enable rotation and, as you did previously, press another key (*X*, *Y*, or *Z*) corresponding to the axis about which you want to rotate the objects. To render image, as shown in Figure 4-16, press *F12*.

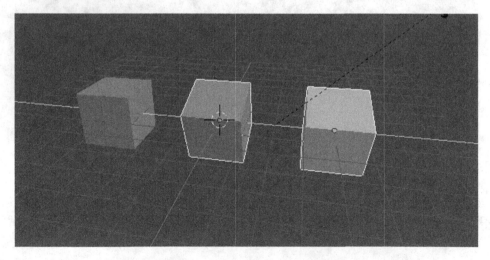

Figure 4-15. Rotating multiple objects

Figure 4-16. Render image

Similarly, you can translate and scale the highlighted objects by pressing the *G* and *S* keys, respectively. Before moving ahead, try transforming multiple objects using various shortcut keys listed in Table 4-1.

Table 4-1. Object Mode Shortcuts

Shortcut	Description
MiddleClick Move	Rotate grid
Shift MiddleClick Move	Translate grid
Ctrl + (OR) WheelUp	Zoom In
A	Toggle "select all"
RightClick	Select object
Shift RightClick	Toggle "multi-select object"
Ctrl I	Invert selection
Ctrl LeftClick Move	Lasso select
G X	Translate object(s) along global X
R X	Rotate object(s) about global X
S X	Scale object(s) along global X
F12	Render image

Modeling Objects for the Game

This section shows how to model objects for the *Tank Fence* game. First, however, you will find it helpful to work through a basic example of editing a mesh. Load a new Blender file from the *Info* window.

Note   Mesh is a primitive shape in Blender that can be used to model various complex shapes. There are various types of meshes in Blender (for example, plane, cube, cone, torus), and, to use a mesh, we must select it from the available meshes from the Add menu in the *Info* window.

To edit meshes by making changes to their geometry (edges, faces, and vertices), we must select the *Edit* mode from the *3D View* header, as shown in Figure 4-5. You can also switch between *Object* and *Edit* modes by pressing *Tab*.

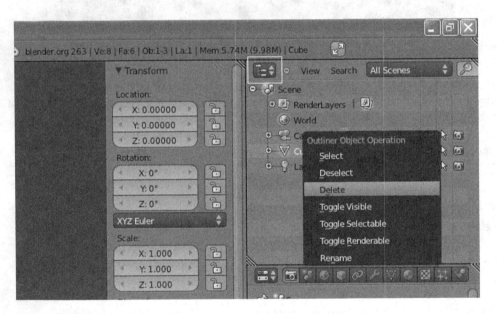

Figure 4-17. Deleting object from the Outliner Window

Note   If you accidentally deleted the cube mesh from the grid, you can add it back again. Snap (crosshair) cursor to the center (Figure 4-18) by pressing *Shift S*, and add the cube mesh by selecting it from Add menu, as shown in Figure 4-19.

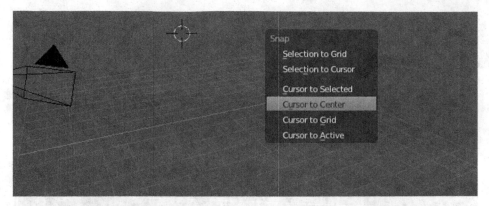

Figure 4-18. Snap cursor to center

Figure 4-19. Adding a mesh

Creating an Equilateral Triangle

In the following example, you must create an equilateral triangle by editing a cube mesh. After loading a new Blender file with cube mesh, start editing this mesh using the following steps:

1. From the *3D View* header, select *View ➤ Navigation ➤ Orbit Left*. This helps move clockwise around the cube mesh, as shown in Figure 4-20.

a. You can also middle-click and drag to rotate the grid.

b. This is useful, as it allows you to view the objects from different angles.

c. Table 4-1 provides more of these shortcuts.

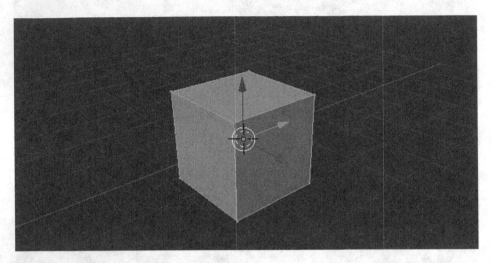

Figure 4-20. Cube mesh in Edit Mode

2. In the *Edit* mode (*Tab*), zoom-in (*Ctrl +*) and press the *Z* key to toggle the Wireframe mode.

a. Wireframe mode makes it easy to get a skeletal view of the mesh, while it is being edited.

b. This makes it easy to select hidden vertices (Figures 4-22 and 4-23), edges, and faces.

c. Wireframe mode can also be selected from the *3D View* header, as shown in Figure 4-21.

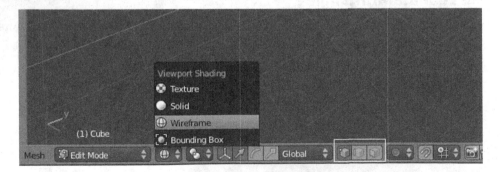

Figure 4-21. 3D View header

3. Toggle "select all" by pressing the *A* key.

   a. The default mesh "select-mode" (in the *Edit* mode) is for vertices. So, when the *A* key is pressed again, all vertices in the cube mesh are selected.

   b. In this default mode, when you use lasso-select to select edges or faces, you aren't able to. Instead, you can only select vertices.

Note   The mesh select-mode is of the following types: *Vertex select*, *Edge select*, and *Face select*.

---

   c. Buttons highlighted in white border in Figure 4-21 are used to switch between mesh select-modes. As stated–previously, the default mode is *Vertex select*.

4. To create an equilateral triangle, lasso-select vertices, as shown in Figure 4-22.

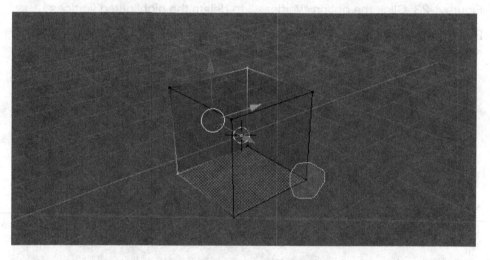

Figure 4-22. Selecting vertices using lasso-select

5. The remaining vertices must be removed (Figure 4-23). Press *Ctrl I* to invert selection.

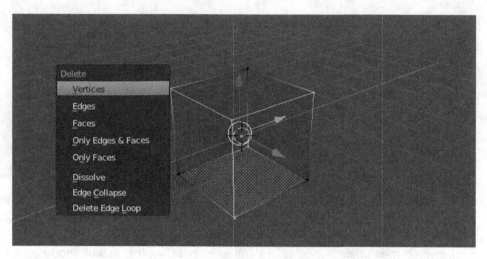

Figure 4-23. *Deleting vertices in Edit Mode*

6. Press *Delete* to display the menu with delete operations, as shown in Figure 4-23. Click the option "Vertices," to delete the highlighted vertices.

7. Press the *A* key to select all vertices. Three vertices are selected (Figure 4-24), representing the corners of the equilateral triangle you must create.

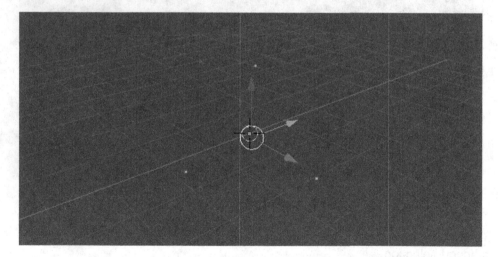

Figure 4-24. *Selecting vertices for creating an equilateral triangle*

8. Finally, press the *F* key to create a face from the selected vertices.

The shape you modeled is an equilateral triangle, shown in Figure 4-25. Toggle the Wireframe mode to get a better look at the object.

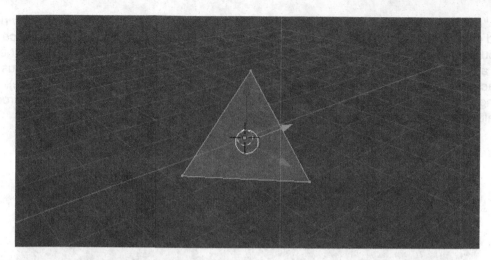

Figure 4-25. Creating a face from vertices

Now, we look at a very interesting feature in the *Edit* mode. To do so, you get a better view across this triangle (Figure 4-26) by orbiting right.

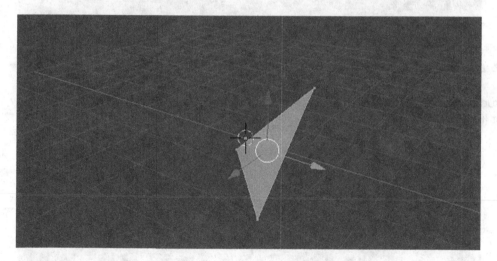

Figure 4-26. Orbiting right of the triangle

> **Note** Orbit right by selecting the option *View* ➤ *Navigation* ➤ *Orbit Right* from the *3D View* header. Recall that you can also middle-click and drag to orbit around the object (by rotating the grid).

Using the "Extrude Region" command, we can extrude and move the current selection. By now, if you tried experimenting with lasso-select and mesh select-modes (*Vertex*, *Edge*, and *Face* select), you should understand that current selection could mean vertices, edges, faces, or objects. Extruding a triangle—like the triangle we created (Figure 4-25)—into a 3D object, requires us to select a face. We select a face by simply right-clicking on it (when in the *Face* select mode). By pressing the *E* key (shortcut key for the "Extrude Region" command, Table 4-2), we extrude this face along its surface-normal, as shown in Figure 4-27.

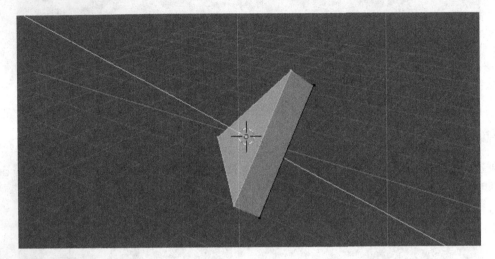

Figure 4-27. Extrude Region

After extruding the equilateral triangle, switch back to the *Object* mode to get a better view of this 3D object (Figure 4-28).

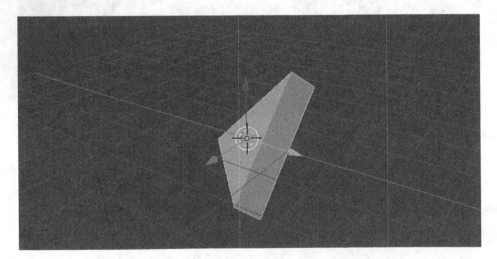

Figure 4-28. Extruded equilateral triangle, Object Mode

tankFence Blender File

Open the `tankFence1.blend` file from the source code for this chapter (`Blender/tankFence1.blend`). It consists of the extruded equilateral triangle you created. The rotation values for the object have been set from the *properties shelf* (highlighted in yellow border in Figure 4-29), so that it becomes (almost) parallel to the grid surface.

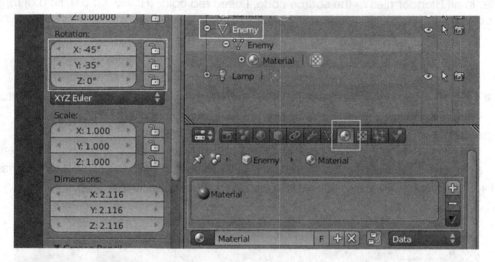

Figure 4-29. Material context in Properties Window

This object represents the enemy, shown in Figure 2-6. Before making more changes to this file, select *View ➤ Top* from the *3D View* header. This aligns the global axes in Blender, along with the *right handed* OpenGL ES coordinate system (Figure 3-17), making it easy to edit the positions of objects added to the world-space of the *3D View*.

Now, continue editing this file. From the *properties shelf*, set the location of this object to {10.0, 10.0, and 0.0} for X, Y, and Z, respectively. This moves the object near the top-right corner of the grid. From the *Outliner* window, double-click the object label "Cube." This allows you to rename the object. Set the name to "Enemy," and press *Enter*. Similarly, rename the cascaded label (along small "plus" button) "Cube" to "Enemy." Click the "plus" button to reveal the object material.

Expand the *Outliner* window by dragging the resizable-cursor. This cursor appears when you position the mouse pointer at the border of any window in Blender. In this case, expand the left border of the *Outliner* window. Windows layed above or below the *Outliner* window are also expanded. Now, turn your attention to the *Properties* window (Figure 4-29).

Material Context

Toggle back to the *Object* mode, and click the *Material context-button* (highlighted in yellow border in Figure 4-29) in the *Properties* window. After making sure that the "Enemy" object is selected, as shown in Figure 4-29, click the "minus" button in the material context to remove the material associated with this object.

We must link a material with this object to color it. To do so, create a new material slot (highlighted in green border in Figure 4-29). Click the "plus" button to create a new material slot. Then, click "New" to add a new material to this slot. Rename this material "Enemy" by over-typing the name "Material.001" (automatically set by Blender). Under the "Diffuse" panel, set the intensity as "1.0." This allows you to clearly observe the material color. Finally, to set this color, click on the white bar directly below the label "Diffuse." This displays a color-picker. Inside, you can also type an RGB color value. In all Blender files in the source code, I used red color (R: 1.0, G: 0.0, B: 0.0) for the "Enemy" object.

> **Note**   The object name in the *Outliner* window, along with two other cascaded names for this object (Figure 4-29), should be identical, including the upper/lower-case alphabets. If the object name is "Cube," the cascaded name should be "Cube," and the next cascaded name (representing the material) should also be "Cube," as shown in Figure 4-30 (in this figure, the object name is "Enemy").
>
> This is a prerequisite for the Perl parser. Basically, having the same names makes it possible for the parser to look for the components associated with the object in .obj and .mtl Blender files.

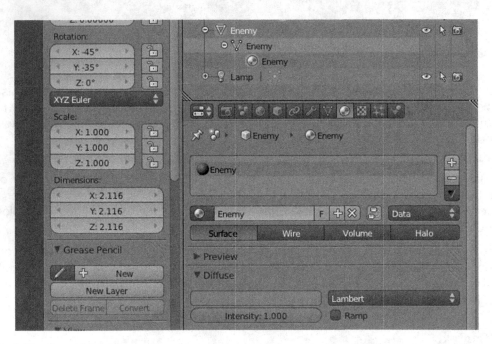

Figure 4-30. Setting the material diffuse-color

Player Object

From the Add menu in the *Info* window, add a cube mesh by selecting *Add* ➤ *Mesh* ➤ *Cube*. Set its labels in the *Outliner* window as "Player", as we did for the "Enemy" object. Next, remove the material associated with this object and create a new material slot. Finally, click "New" to add a new material to this slot. As we did previously, set the material name as the object name. After setting the diffuse intensity as "1.0", set the RGB color as (0.0, 0.0, 1.0).

Adding Plane Mesh

As shown in Figure 2-6, *Tank Fence* also contains a plane region. The player has to guard this region. You may already understand how to add this plane in Blender. Try it yourself. Open the tankFence3.blend file from the source code for this chapter. This file contains all the changes you have made so far. It also contains this plane mesh (scaled to "10.0" along X and Y), with an incorrect material name. After setting the material name to "Plane", start editing the cube ("Player") object.

Editing the Player Object

To make it easy to view this object, toggle the visibility of other object(s) in the world-space by clicking the (corresponding) "eye" image-button in the *Outliner* window.

Now, we discuss how to make this cube look like a tank (at least somewhat!). The easiest way to do so is by extruding any lateral surface of a cube and then scaling-down the extrusion. The way this is exactly performed in Blender, however, is a little different.

After editing the tankFence3.blend file (for material name), rotate the grid to get a configuration similar to Figure 4-31. Recall that you can do so by middle-clicking and then dragging the mouse to rotate the grid.

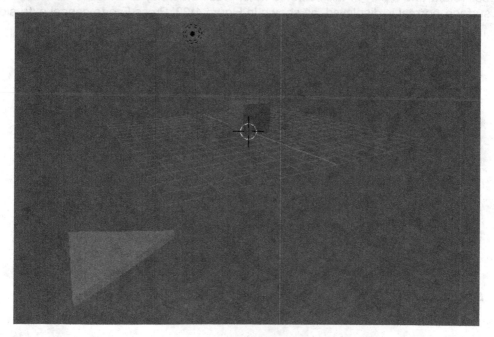

Figure 4-31. Configuring the grid surface

After obtaining a configuration similar to Figure 4-31, zoom in. Then, from the *3D View* header, select the *Face* select-mode. This allows you to select any face for extrusion. Select the front-face, pointed by the (crosshair) cursor, as shown in Figure 4-32. You can lasso-select this face or right-click on it to select it.

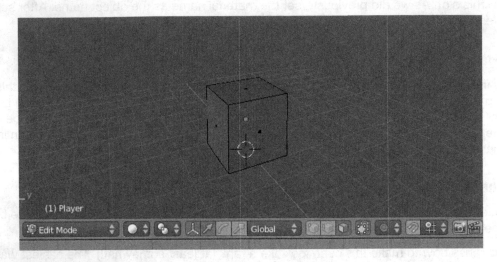

Figure 4-32. Mesh select-mode: Face

You do not have to extrude an entire face of a cube. Doing so will only result in a cuboid. To create a shape similar to a tank, extrude only a part of this selected face. The extrusion tool can be used for this purpose. To extrude a part of this selected face, press the *E* key to enable extrusion. The axis along the surface-normal is displayed, as shown in Figure 4-33. Press *Esc* to cancel extrusion.

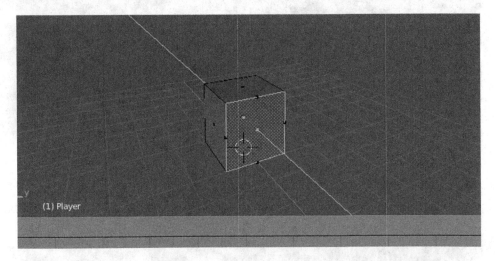

Figure 4-33. Extruding the face

This creates an extra face at the top of the selected face. Blender automatically makes this new face the current selected face. Next, press the *S* key to scale this face. Scale it inward (Figure 4-34) so you can then extrude it—to look like a tank gun.

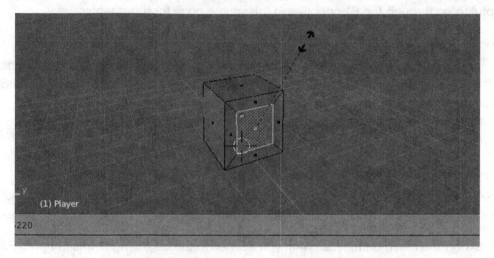

Figure 4-34. Scaling face inward

Finally, after scaling the face, press the *E* key to extrude it, as shown in Figure 4-35. Recall that extrusion takes place along surface-normal. So, unlike translation, there is no need to specify any axis for extrusion.

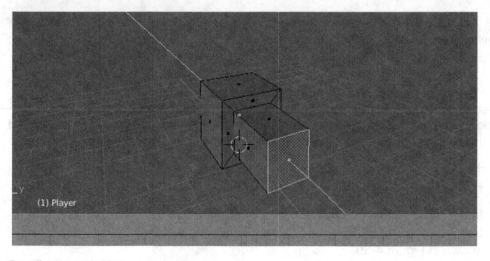

Figure 4-35. Extruding the scaled face

Exporting Mesh Data

Now that you have seen the modeling of objects for *Tank Fence*, we discuss how to export the mesh data to .obj files. If you had difficulty understanding the examples previously discussed, you may find it helpful to go through the Blender files in the source code for this chapter.

> **Note**   .obj is a geometry definition file format first developed by *Wavefront Technologies*. This file format is a simple data-format that represents 3D geometry alone—namely, the position of each vertex, normals, faces (that make each polygon defined as a list of vertices), and texture-vertices. The .mtl file format is a companion file format that describes surface shading (material) properties of objects within one or more .obj files.
>
> You can read more about these file formats at http://en.wikipedia.org/wiki/Wavefront_.obj_file.

Before we export the mesh data, recall what you learned in the beginning of this chapter. Based on what we've already discussed, you should understand that the kind of mesh data we have to export should be composed of triangles.

Blender makes it very easy to "triangulate" faces of an object. To do so, after selecting the object, toggle to *Edit* mode. Then, press *Ctrl T* to triangulate faces. That's all!

> **Note**   Although the default (mesh) select-mode is *Vertex select*, Blender understands that you want to triangulate faces.

Now, open the tankFence5.blend file from the source code for this chapter (Blender/tankFence5.blend). It consists of all the game objects you created. If you toggle to *Edit* mode, observe that all the objects (that is, faces of objects) are already triangulated. To export this file as .obj (and accompanying .mtl) format, complete the following steps:

1. To ensure the required "Import-Export" add-on is available, select the option "User Preferences" under File menu.

2. In the "User Preferences" editor, click the *Context* button corresponding to the "Addons". Then, from the "Categories" panel, select "Import-Export", as shown in Figure 4-36.

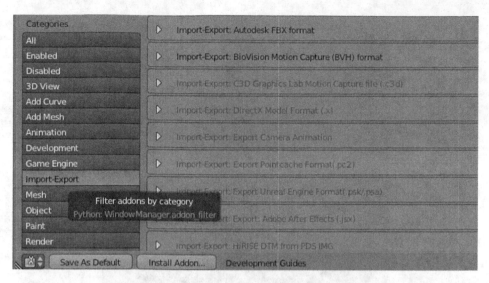

Figure 4-36. User Preferences: Addons

3. Scroll down the available list of add-ons to find the add-on corresponding to .obj format. It should be named similar to "Wavefront obj format".

4. Check this add-on to enable it in Blender. This allows you to export the mesh data to .obj files. Finally, close this editor.

5. Under File menu, select *Export ➤ Wavefront (.obj)*.

6. From the "Export-Obj" panel, check the option "Include Normals". Set "Forward:" and "Up:" as "Y Forward" and "Z Up", respectively.

7. Save this configuration (changes made in step 6) by clicking the "plus" button, alongside the select-list "Operator Presets" (Figure 4-37).

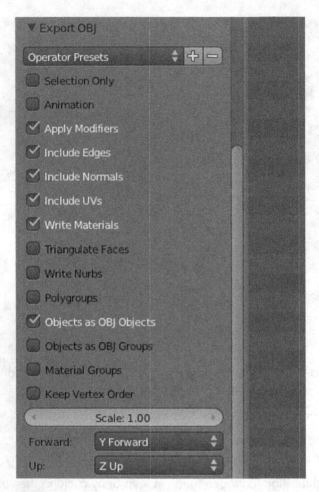

Figure 4-37. Export-Obj panel

8. Finally, click the "Export Obj" button. This exports the mesh data to `.obj` file.
    Another file (`.mtl`) accompanies `.obj` file. *Obj* or object-file-format contains
    geometry definitions for various objects, whereas *Mtl* or material-file-format
    contains material colors for these objects.

Table 4-2. Edit Mode Shortcuts

Shortcut	Description
Ctrl Tab	Switch mesh select-mode
Ctrl T	Triangulate Faces
Ctrl Z	Undo last operation
Ctrl Shift Z	Redo operation
Z	Toggle Wireframe mode
F	Make Face
E	Extrude Region
RightClick	Select single vertex, edge or face
Shift RightClick	Multi-select vertex, edge or face
Delete	Show Delete menu
G X	Translate selection along global X
R X	Rotate selection about global X
S X	Scale selection along global X

Parsing Objects for OpenGL ES

Now, we demonstrate the use of a Perl (.obj) parser to parse the triangulated mesh data in .obj files. This parser is still in its early stages (it does not support textures for objects), but it has sufficient functionality to collect the following data from .obj (and .mtl) files:

- It can collect basic data about objects, such as names and materials.

- Listing 4-9 contains a few lines from the beginning of the file tankFence5.obj, whereas Listing 4-10 contains a few lines from the file tankFence5.mtl (you exported these files using tankFence5.blend file).

Listing 4-9. Chapter4/Blender/tankFence5.obj

```
# Blender v2.63 (sub 0) OBJ File: 'tankFence5.blend'
# www.blender.org
mtllib tankFence5.mtl
o Plane
v 10.000000 -10.000000 0.000000
v -10.000000 -10.000000 0.000000
v 10.000000 10.000000 0.000000
v -10.000000 10.000000 0.000000
vn 0.000000 0.000000 1.000000
usemtl Plane
s off
f 3//1 4//1 2//1
f 1//1 3//1 2//1
```

Listing 4-10. Chapter4/Blender/tankFence5.mtl

```
# Blender MTL File: 'tankFence5.blend'
# Material Count: 3
newmtl Enemy
Ns 96.078431
Ka 0.000000 0.000000 0.000000
Kd 1.000000 0.000000 0.000000
Ks 0.500000 0.500000 0.500000
Ni 1.000000
d 1.000000
illum 2

newmtl Plane
Ns 96.078431
Ka 0.000000 0.000000 0.000000
Kd 1.000000 1.000000 1.000000
Ks 0.500000 0.500000 0.500000
Ni 1.000000
d 1.000000
illum 2
```

- Recall the names of objects you modeled–Plane, Enemy, and Player. Listing 4-9 contains the block of data for Plane object. Perl parser stores object names (for example, "Plane", "Enemy") and uses them to read the material file to get the material colors. So, corresponding to the Plane object, it stores white color—indicated as "Kd 1.000000 1.000000 1.000000" (RGB format) in Listing 4-10.

- It can collect mesh data for triangle meshes, such that this data is ready for use with glDrawElements with mode GL_TRIANGLES.

- glDrawElements with mode GL_TRIANGLES requires a float array with unique vertices (representing a shape) and element indices (representing triangle meshes) for this float array.

- Perl parser stores unique object vertices. These vertices are listed (Listing 4-9) below object name (for example, "o Plane") as "v vx vy vz".

- Element indices are also stored. *Obj* format makes it easy for the parser to find element indices, representing meshes.

- Face definitions (Listing 4-9) "f 3 4 2" already contain vertex indices, representing meshes. The set {3, 4, 2} represents a triangle mesh with vertices v3, v4, and v2 (v1 is the first vertex that appears in .obj file, v2 is the second vertex, and so on).

- The kind of face definition this parser searches for should also contain normal indices. Normal indices are included in face definitions after double slashes. Normals are included as "vn 0.000000 0.000000 1.000000".

- For advanced programming in OpenGL ES, such as the computation of shading values, this parser also stores normals corresponding to the triangle meshes (that is, per-face normals).

- For every vertex of an object, it also calculates the normalized average of adjacent normals. This makes the shading effects smooth.

- The material names should be the same as that of the corresponding object names.

- When these conditions are met, parser takes the name of Blender file and parses the corresponding .obj and .mtl files. Finally, it produces a text file as its output. This file contains mesh data that can be readily used with glDrawElements with mode GL_TRIANGLES.

> **Note**   tankFence5.obj and tankFence5.mtl files are also available in the source code for this chapter. You can open and read through them in your favorite text editor to understand more about *Obj* and *Mtl* mesh data. Do not modify them!

Installing Perl

To get this parser into action, your system requires a Perl (version 5) installation. Of course, if you are on a *nix system, Perl comes pre-installed. There are eight steps to install Perl on Windows 7:

> **Note**   Perl (version 5) comes pre-installed with most *nix systems, so there is nothing to install or configure. After creating a Perl script (for example, program.pl), you must add execute permissions to run it. From shell, run "chmod +x program.pl". Now, to run this script, you can simply type "program.pl".
>
> If you are launching the script by running "perl program.pl", the script does not need execute permissions. If, however, you are executing it using "program.pl" or "./program.pl", it does need execute permissions.

1. For this demonstration, we use *ActivePerl*—a closed-source distribution of Perl from *ActiveState*. (You can read more about *ActiveState* at http://en.wikipedia.org/wiki/ActiveState.) Download the *ActivePerl* installer corresponding to your system from www.activestate.com/activeperl. I downloaded the installer highlighted in Figure 4-38, as I have 32-bit Windows 7.

Download Perl: Other Platforms and Versions

Version	Windows (x86)	Windows (64-bit, x64)	Mac OS X (Universal)	Linux (x86)
5.16.2.1602	Windows Installer (MSI)	Windows Installer (MSI)	Mac Disk Image (DMG)	AS Packa
5.14.3.1404	Windows Installer (MSI)	Windows Installer (MSI)	Mac Disk Image (DMG)	AS Packa

Figure 4-38. ActivePerl installers

2. After the installer has downloaded, select it from the downloads folder (Figure 4-39) and double-click it. You may see *User Account Control* dialog after this. If so, click "Yes".

Figure 4-39. Selecting the installer from downloads folder

3. Next, click "Run" in the *Security Warning* window, as shown in Figure 4-40.

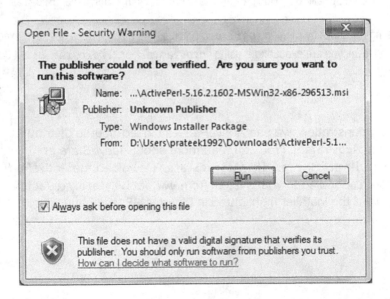

Figure 4-40. Security-warning window

4. Click "Next" in the *ActivePerl Setup Wizard* (Figure 4-41).

Figure 4-41. ActivePerl Setup Wizard

5. Accept the license agreement and click "Next."

6. In the *Custom Setup* window, set the installation location and click "Next." As Figure 4-42 illustrates, I install *ActivePerl* under "D:\."

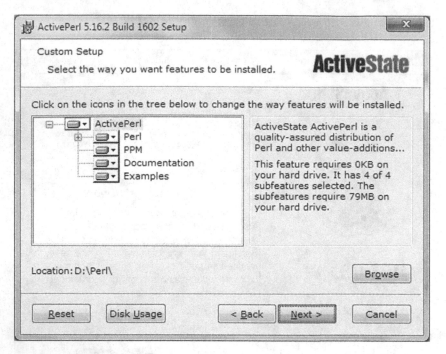

Figure 4-42. ActivePerl Setup Wizard: Custom Setup

7. In the *Setup Options* window (Figure 4-43), leave everything to the default settings and click "Next."

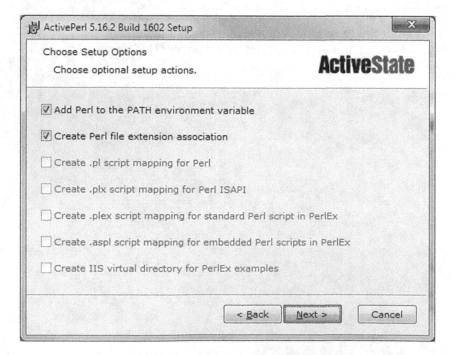

Figure 4-43. ActivePerl Setup Wizard: Setup Options

8. Finally, click "Finish" (Figure 4-44) to complete the setup.

Figure 4-44. Complete the setup

Once you have installed *ActivePerl*, you see the folder "D:\Perl" (assuming you installed *ActivePerl* under "D:\"). This folder contains native binary distributions of Perl for Windows. Next, let's see how you can get the parser.

Downloading Parser

You can download the Perl (mesh) parser from my Bitbucket account—
`https://bitbucket.org/prateekmehta`. Click on the repository "blender_obj_perl_parser_bitbucket". Next, click the download link from the "repo-stats" section, as shown in Figure 4-45. This downloads the archive file `prateekmehta-blender_obj_perl_parser_bitbucket-2cb343b9e1a5.zip`. Now, move this file in a folder of your choice, and then extract it. I extract it under "D:\". This creates the folder "D:\prateekmehta-blender_obj_perl_parser_bitbucket-2cb343b9e1a5", with contents as shown in Figure 4-46.

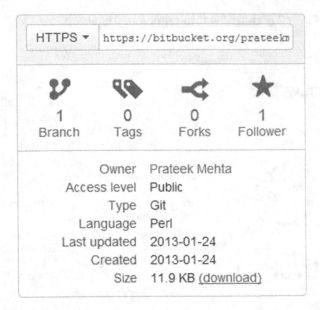

Figure 4-45. *Downloading parser*

Figure 4-46. *Extracted parser*

This folder contains the main parser file—`parser.pl`—and another Perl file, inside the "Utility" folder. The `parser.txt` file contains mesh data from a Blender file. It contains both *Obj* and *Mtl* data. This text file is provided so you can go through the structuring of (input) data (*Obj* and *Mtl*), which is necessarily required by the parser.

Now, create a folder "Blender," and copy the *Obj* and *Mtl* files from the source code for this chapter from section "Exporting mesh data" (Figure 4-47) into it. I copy these files under "D:\Blender."

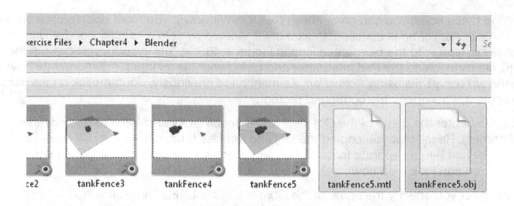

Figure 4-47. *Selecting Obj and Mtl files*

Using the Parser

To use this parser, you must provide correct paths to a couple of necessary files. So, open the `parser.pl` file in a text editor of your choice to make the following changes:

1. In line 40, replace the string value for scalar $obj_file_parent_path with the full path for the folder in which you have copied the Obj and Mtl files. On Windows, if the folder containing these files is "Blender" and is directly under "D:\", then line 40 should be set to $obj_file_parent_path = "D:/Blender/";. Similarly, if you are on a *nix system, inside your home directory (/home/username/), and the Obj and Mtl files are inside /home/username/Blender/, set the value of scalar $obj_file_parent_path as "home/username/Blender/".

2. In line 326, replace the path (only the path, not the scalars with white spaces—" $rx $ry $rz") inside backticks with full path to the `precision.pl` file, that is, if you moved the folder (prateekmehta-blender_obj_perl_parser_bitbucket-2cb343b9e1a5) with Perl files directly under "D:\", then line 326 should be set to @output=`D:\\prateekmehta-blender_obj_perl_parser_bitbucket-2cb343b9e1a5\\Utility\\precision.pl $rx $ry $rz`;. Similarly, proceed in a suitable way if you are on a *nix system.

Note If you are on a Windows system with *ActivePerl* installed, you may also remove the first line—"#!C:/wamp/bin/perl/bin/perl.exe"–from the `parser.pl` file. It will not affect the output.

If you are on a *nix system and relying on the executable permission to work for you, you must modify this line to point to your local Perl path.

After making these edits, you can parse mesh files. On Windows, you must double-click on the parser.pl file (if *ActivePerl* is installed) to execute it. *ActivePerl* sets a special icon for files with .pl extensions, similar to the blue-green icon in Figure 4-46. On *nix system, you can run the parser.pl file by invoking the Perl interpreter and giving your file as input. I demonstrate how to execute the parser.pl file using *ActivePerl*. As mentioned previously, double-click on the parser.pl file to execute it. This opens the command prompt.

Now, you must enter the name of the *Obj* file—"tankFence5" (*Obj* and *Mtl* files should have identical names). Recall that you copied the *Obj* and *Mtl* files (Figure 4-47)—tankFence5.obj and tankFence5.mtl—to a separate folder. Since you specified the path of this folder (when editing parser.pl), Perl can look it up now.

Press *Enter* after you specify the name of the *Obj* file (Figure 4-48). Then, click "Open" in the *Security Warning* window (if you are on a Windows 7 system), as shown in Figure 4-49. You may also uncheck the checkbox in this window. This allows the parser to execute without waiting for confirmation.

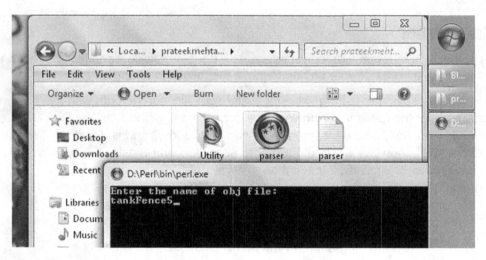

Figure 4-48. Command prompt: Specifying the Obj file

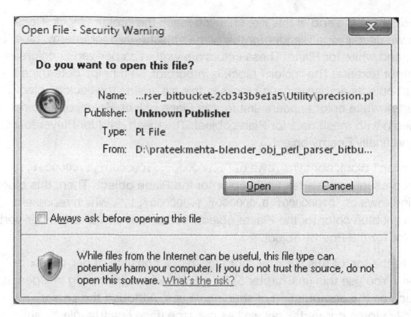

Figure 4-49. Security-warning window: Unchecking confirmation

When the parser has executed, you can get back to the folder in which you copied the *Obj* and *Mtl* files. You will observe a new file inside this folder (Figure 4-50). This is the output of the parser, a text file that contains mesh data, ready for use with `glDrawElements` with mode `GL_TRIANGLES`.

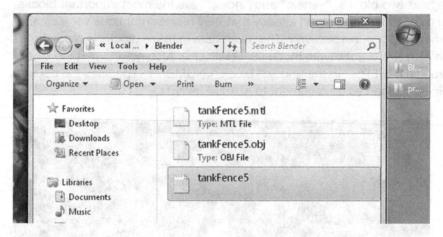

Figure 4-50. Output text file

Using the Mesh Data

Before we discuss how to use the contents of this output text file, we describe the blocks of mesh data inside this file. So, open the file `tankFence5.txt` in your favorite text editor and start reading through.

1. Scroll down at the end of this file, until you reach the "color:" block. Recall the colors we used inside Blender for the game objects—red for Enemy, blue for Player, and white for Plane. These colors are written as per-vertex colors in the output text file. The "color:" block is important, as it helps determine the order of objects across various blocks in this file. Inside the "color:" block, per-vertex white color appears first for the Plane object. So, all other blocks also begin with mesh data for Plane object. The mesh data for Player follows this, and finally Enemy object.

2. The "color:" block contains rows of "1.000000f,1.000000f,1.000000f,1," ; this represents per-vertex white color for the Plane object. Then, this block contains rows of "0.000000f,0.000000f,1.000000f,1,", which represent per-vertex blue color for the Player object. Similarly, it contains the per-vertex red color for the Enemy object.

3. Scroll to the top of this file. The "normal:" block consists of per-vertex normals. You use this (in Chapter 5) for advanced programming in OpenGL ES, such as the computation of shading values. Although the parser internally stores per-vertex, as well as per-face (face is a triangle mesh) normals, it uses the per-face normals when averaging normals adjacent to a vertex normal. The output shown in this block is the averages of these face normals adjacent to per-vertex normals. Note again that the mesh data in every block follows the same order as in the "color:" block.

4. The next two blocks, "vertex:" and "index:", are the most important blocks. You must have understood already that they represent unique vertices and element indices, respectively. The mesh data in these blocks is ready for use with glDrawElements (with mode GL_TRIANGLES). Also note that in the label "size:<NUMBER>" in the "index:" block, <NUMBER> specifies the count of indices, passed as an argument to glDrawElements.

Figure 4-51. TANK FENCE ELEMENTS 1: Player object

The section "Drawing line and triangle primitives" discussed using glDrawElements with mode GL_TRIANGLES. It also talked about the *GL TRIANGLE ELEMENTS* application (Chapter4/gltriangleelements.zip) to render triangle primitives, as shown in Figure 4-2. Similar to this application, there are three other applications (in the source code for this chapter)—*TANK FENCE ELEMENTS 1, 2, and 3*—in which the use of parser's output text file has been demonstrated. Now, we explain the first application–*TANK FENCE ELEMENTS 1*. The others build up from this application to add per-vertex color (using the block "color:" from the output text file), as well as Plane and Enemy objects (Figures 4-52 and 4-53 show their outputs).

Figure 4-52. TANK FENCE ELEMENTS 2: Using color from output text file

Figure 4-53. TANK FENCE ELEMENTS 3: Adding other objects

Adding the Player Object

The Main class in the *TANK FENCE ELEMENTS 1* application is identical to the Main class from the *TOUCH ROTATION* application (Figure 2-16), inside the source code for Chapter 2. This class provides the angle of rotation to rotate the rendered object.

The Renderer class (GLES20Renderer) is also similar to the one we created at the beginning of this chapter. The only difference is the naming convention (for example, _tankProgram in place of _triangleProgram) and the field _tankUMVPLocation. _tankUMVPLocation is the location of uniform variable uMVP (of type mat4). Recall that this matrix is used to transform the vertices of the rendered object, in this case, the vertices of the tank (that is, the Player object you modeled in Blender).

Now, turn your attention to the inittank method in the Renderer class. Also open the file tankFence5.txt (parser's output) in any text editor. In the tankFence5.txt file, scroll down to the block "vertex:". As mentioned previously, the mesh data in every block follows the same order as in the "color:" block. So, the following set of vertices in the tankFence5.txt file corresponds to the vertex float array for the Plane object:

```
10.000000f,-10.000000f,0.000000f,
-10.000000f,-10.000000f,0.000000f,
10.000000f,10.000000f,0.000000f,
-10.000000f,10.000000f,0.000000f,
```

Similarly, the set of vertices from "-1.562685f,-2.427994f,0.000000f," to "0.781342f,3.437026f, 1.500000f," corresponds to the vertex float array for the Player object (that is, the tank initialized in the inittank method). The float array tankVFA (in the inittank method) is composed of these vertices, and they have been copied from the "vertex:" block in the output text file.

Below this block, the "index:" block contains indices, representing triangle meshes. The following sets of indices correspond to the index short array for the Plane object:

```
2,3,1,
0,2,1,
```

Similarly, the sets of indices from "4,5,1," to "14,10,15," correspond to the index short array for the Player object. The short array tankISA (in the inittank method) is composed of these indices; they have been copied from the "index:" block. As discussed, the label "size:<NUMBER>" above this set specifies the count of indices to be passed as an argument to glDrawElements:

```
size:84
4,5,1,
..
14,10,15,
```

The label "size:84" in the "index:" block specifies the count of indices for the Player object (please note that the Player object is the tank initialized in the inittank method). Because of this, in the onDrawFrame method, the following call is made:
GLES20.glDrawElements(GLES20.GL_TRIANGLES, 84, GLES20.GL_UNSIGNED_SHORT, _tankISB);.

In Figure 4-51 (screen shot from the *TANK FENCE ELEMENTS 1* application), the color of the tank is made yellow by directly writing to the gl_FragColor shader variable—gl_FragColor = vec4(1.0,1.0,0.0,1);. Instead of directly writing to this variable, the application *TANK FENCE ELEMENTS 2* includes the per-vertex colors copied from the "color:" block at the bottom of tankFence5.txt file (recall that, while modeling the tank, we colored it blue—Figure 4-35). By now, you should understand the kind of shader variables used for this purpose—an *attribute* variable (say aColor) and a *varying* variable (say vColor), each of type vec4. The *TANK FENCE ELEMENTS 3* application adds other objects–Plane and Enemy. It is left as an exercise for you to go through this application.

Basic Components in the Blender Interface: Screenshots

This additional section provides screen shots for the five basic components in Blender.

Figure 4-54 shows the *Info* window. It is positioned at the top of the Blender interface. As previously explained, it consists of useful menus, such as File, Add, and Help.

Figure 4-54. Info Window

Figure 4-55 shows the 3D Window, also known as the *3D View* (window). The 3D Window is where we spend most of our time in Blender. In this window, we can rearrange the objects and edit their individual vertices. We can also define animation. This window is positioned at the center of the Blender interface.

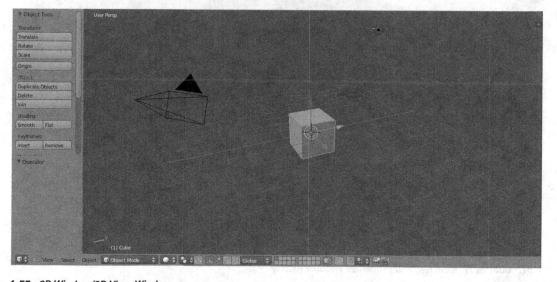

Figure 4-55. 3D Window/3D View Window

Figure 4-56 shows the *Timeline* window. It is positioned at the bottom of the Blender interface. As you may have guessed, *Timeline* is the core of the animation process in Blender. It is most often used to scrub animations.

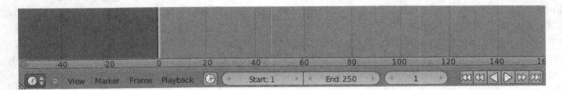

Figure 4-56. Timeline Window

Figure 4-57 shows the *Outliner* window (up) and the *Properties* window (down). The *Outliner* window is used for selecting, deleting, and hiding objects modeled in a scene. As previously discussed, the *Properties* window displays panels of functions. The *Outliner* window is positioned at the upper-right corner of the Blender interface, and the *Properties* window is positioned at the lower-right corner.

Figure 4-57. Outliner Window (up) and Properties Window (down)

> **Note**   Scenes are a very useful tool for managing your projects. The cube mesh in the empty space you see when you open Blender for the first time is the default scene. (You can read more on scenes at `http://wiki.blender.org/index.php/Doc:2.6/Manual/Interface/Scenes`.)

Summary

This chapter introduced the ES 2.0 function `glDrawElements`, which helps avoid the redundancy of mesh data. It demonstrated the basic use of Blender, the open-source 3D content creation suite. It also discussed the use of a parser to create ready to use mesh data from Blender *Obj* files. Finally, this chapter showed how to use this data inside ES 2.0 applications.

Chapter 5 considers two common ways to enhance the look of our ES 2.0 applications—using textures and lighting/shading effects.

Texturing and Shading

In this chapter, you will learn about two common ways to enhance the look of our ES 2.0 applications — texturing and shading. First, I will talk about using single textures and then I will show you how you can combine textures with colors. After this, you will learn using multiple textures with rendered objects. Finally, I will discuss lighting and shading effects in ES 2.0, which are achieved using our own logic for the interaction between surface and light sources.

Vertex Buffer Objects

The per-vertex data, specified (for rendering objects) using arrays, is stored in the main memory; however, when a call to glDraw* (glDrawArrays or glDrawElements) is made, this data must be copied from the main memory to the GPU memory.

To avoid this we can use vertex buffer objects, which help to cache the vertex data in GPU memory. This can significantly reduce power consumption, as well as the transfer of data from main memory to GPU memory, which is otherwise incurred if we do not use these buffer objects.

Types of Buffer Objects

There are two types of vertex buffer objects—*array buffer objects* and *element array buffer objects*. The *array buffer objects* are used to cache the per-vertex data, such as vertices {x, y, z}, colors {r, g, b, a}, normals {Nx, Ny, Nz}, and so on, and the *element array buffer objects* are used to cache the corresponding indices of these arrays.

Using Buffer Objects

To use buffer objects, we first need to generate them. To do this, call the method GLES20.glGenBuffers. This method has two overloaded versions. The one we use here takes three arguments:

- The first argument specifies the number of buffer objects that must be generated.

- The second argument specifies the array to store the returned (integer) ids, representing objects. Please note that the id "0" is reserved by OpenGL ES.

- The third argument specifies the offset of type int. For all examples discussed, we set this argument to "0", meaning "no-offset".

After generating buffer object(s), call the method GLES20.glBindBuffer. This method is used to make a buffer object the current *array buffer object* or the current *element array buffer object*.

So, depending on the use of the buffer object, the first argument passed to this method is either GLES20.GL_ARRAY_BUFFER or GLES20.GL_ELEMENT_ARRAY_BUFFER. The second argument passed to this method is the id of the buffer object, as shown in Listing 5-1. Here, _tankBuffers is an int array of size 2. The size is 2, because we need two buffer objects.

> **Note**   Do not confuse OpenGL ES buffer objects with java.nio.*Buffer objects, such as java.nio.
> ShortBuffer, java.nio.FloatBuffer, and so on.

Listing 5-1. TANK FENCE 1/src/com/apress/android/tankfence1/GLES20Renderer.java

```
GLES20.glGenBuffers(2, _tankBuffers, 0);
GLES20.glBindBuffer(GLES20.GL_ARRAY_BUFFER, _tankBuffers[0]);
GLES20.glBufferData(GLES20.GL_ARRAY_BUFFER, tankVFA.length * 4, _tankVFB, GLES20.GL_STATIC_DRAW);
GLES20.glBindBuffer(GLES20.GL_ELEMENT_ARRAY_BUFFER, _tankBuffers[1]);
GLES20.glBufferData(GLES20.GL_ELEMENT_ARRAY_BUFFER, tankISA.length * 2, _tankISB, GLES20.GL_STATIC_
DRAW);
```

Finally, after making a buffer object the current buffer object, we need to pass it the corresponding vertex or index data using the ES 2.0 function glBufferData. As shown in Listing 5-1, after the call to glBindBuffer(GLES20.GL_ARRAY_BUFFER, _tankBuffers[0]), glBufferData is called, with arguments "GLES20.GL_ARRAY_BUFFER", "tankVFA.length * 4", "_tankVFB", and "GLES20.GL_STATIC_DRAW".

As with glBindBuffer, the first argument passed to glBufferData is either GL_ARRAY_BUFFER or GL_ELEMENT_ARRAY_BUFFER, denoting the target/type of the buffer object. The second argument denotes the size of array (of per-vertex or index data) in bytes. The third argument denotes the Buffer (java.nio.Buffer) for the corresponding vertex or index data. Finally, the last argument can be any one of the following values:

- GL_STATIC_DRAW

- GL_DYNAMIC_DRAW

- GL_STREAM_DRAW

These values are defined as static constants in the android.opengl.GLES20 class. They provide a hint to OpenGL ES on how the application is going to use the data stored in the buffer object. Of these values, GL_STATIC_DRAW and GL_DYNAMIC_DRAW are most commonly used.

As the name suggests, GL_STATIC_DRAW is used when the application does not modify the data stored in the buffer object, whereas GL_DYNAMIC_DRAW is used when the buffer object data is specified repeatedly by the application (and used many times to draw primitives). In the context of the *Tank Fence* game, only missiles use the GL_DYNAMIC_DRAW buffer usage. The buffer object corresponding to missiles undergoes rewrites in a repeated manner, so as to update the vertex data (and the corresponding indices) representing the centers of missiles. The remaining objects in this game (that is, the plane, enemy, and player) use the GL_STATIC_DRAW buffer usage.

> **Note**   We will work with the missile objects in Chapter 6. They are introduced here so you can understand the GL_DYNAMIC_DRAW buffer usage.

So far, we've only looked at how buffer objects are generated and then filled with corresponding data. We still have not discussed the way in which buffer objects' data is passed to the *shaders* (to be specific, a vertex shader). Listing 5-2 shows that doing so is quite easy and almost similar to how you have been passing data (per-vertex and index data) without the use of buffer objects.

Passing a buffer object's data (to the *shaders*) also requires you to make this buffer object the current buffer object, by calling glBindBuffer, as shown in Listing 5-2. Then, call glVertexAttribPointer to tell OpenGL about the format and source of our vertex array data (as discussed in Chapter 3). Finally, call glEnableVertexAttribArray to activate the given attribute location. You may have noticed that the call to glVertexAttribPointer (Listing 5-2) no longer requires you to explicitly specify the FloatBuffer (java.nio.FloatBuffer). This is because calling glBindBuffer makes the specified buffer object (as in this case, *array buffer object*) the current buffer object. Similarly, glDrawElements does not require you to explicitly specify the ShortBuffer (corresponding to the *element array buffer object*), if you assigned it as the current buffer object, as shown in Listing 5-2. So, in place of FloatBuffer or ShortBuffer, argument "0" is passed when calling glVertexAttribPointer or glDrawElements.

Listing 5-2. TANK FENCE 1/src/com/apress/android/tankfence1/GLES20Renderer.java

```
GLES20.glUseProgram(_tankProgram);
GLES20.glUniformMatrix4fv(_tankUMVPLocation, 1, false, _MVPMatrix, 0);
GLES20.glBindBuffer(GLES20.GL_ARRAY_BUFFER, _tankBuffers[0]);
GLES20.glVertexAttribPointer(_tankAPositionLocation, 3, GLES20.GL_FLOAT, false, 12, 0);
GLES20.glEnableVertexAttribArray(_tankAPositionLocation);
GLES20.glBindBuffer(GLES20.GL_ELEMENT_ARRAY_BUFFER, _tankBuffers[1]);
GLES20.glDrawElements(GLES20.GL_TRIANGLES, 84, GLES20.GL_UNSIGNED_SHORT, 0);
```

To understand this better, import the archive file Chapter5/tankfence1.zip. This loads the *TANK FENCE 1* application into your Eclipse workspace. You will also find other similar applications in the source code - *TANK FENCE 2* and *TANK FENCE 3*. These three applications will help you move in a stepwise manner to use buffer objects for the plane, enemy, and player (game objects in the *Tank Fence* game). The outputs of these applications are similar to the *TANK FENCE ELEMENTS* * series of applications. The only difference between these applications is the use of buffer objects.

Using Color Masks

Before moving further, I will also talk about using color masks in ES 2.0. Color masks allow you to enable or disable writes to specific components (red, green, blue, and alpha) in the color buffer.

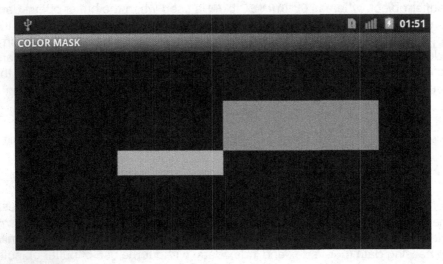

Figure 5-1. Using color masks

You can set color masks using the ES 2.0 function glColorMask. This function takes four Boolean arguments, where each argument corresponds to the "writable" state of a component in the color buffer. To use this function correctly, color mask(s) should be set before each call to any glDraw* function.

To understand this function, consider the following example. Suppose you render two rectangles—rectangleOne (cyan colored) and rectangleTwo (white colored)—and you want to render only the green component of rectangleOne and the red component of rectangleTwo.

To make this work, before you render each of these rectangles (by calling any of glDraw* ES 2.0 functions) using their separate programs, you must set the color masks in the following manner:

- For rectangleOne, set the color mask by calling GLES20.glColorMask(false, true, false, true). Since the green and alpha components are enabled, only the green color will be visible.

- For rectangleTwo, set the color mask by calling GLES20.glColorMask(true, false, false, true). Since the red and alpha components are enabled, only the red color will be visible.

> **Note**   Recall that you can set a single color for the rendered object by directly writing to the built-in *shader* variable—gl_FragColor. To set white color for the rendered object, write the vec4 - (1.0, 1.0, 1.0, 1) to the gl_FragColor variable. Similarly, to set cyan color, write the vec4 - (0.0, 1.0, 1.0, 1).

To demonstrate this, import the application *GL MASK* (Chapter5/glmask.zip) into your Eclipse workspace. This application is almost identical to the *GL RECTANGLE* application in the source code for Chapter 3, except for the Renderer class in *GL MASK* application, which renders two rectangles (Figure 5-1) instead of just one.

Listing 5-3 contains lines of code (from the *GL MASK* application) to set color masks for two rectangles. Please note that, to avoid the first call to glColorMask affecting the color masks set for the second rectangle, color masks for all components are reset by calling glColorMask(true, true, true, true).

Listing 5-3. GL MASK/src/com/apress/android/glmask/GLES20Renderer.java

```
GLES20.glUseProgram(_rectangleTwoProgram);
GLES20.glVertexAttribPointer(_rectangleTwoAVertexLocation, 3, GLES20.GL_FLOAT, false,
0, _rectangleTwoVFB);
GLES20.glEnableVertexAttribArray(_rectangleTwoAVertexLocation);
GLES20.glColorMask(false, true, false, true);
GLES20.glDrawArrays(GLES20.GL_TRIANGLES, 0, 6);
GLES20.glColorMask(true, true, true, true);

GLES20.glUseProgram(_rectangleOneProgram);
GLES20.glVertexAttribPointer(_rectangleOneAVertexLocation, 3, GLES20.GL_FLOAT, false,
0, _rectangleOneVFB);
GLES20.glEnableVertexAttribArray(_rectangleOneAVertexLocation);
GLES20.glColorMask(true, false, false, true);
GLES20.glDrawArrays(GLES20.GL_TRIANGLES, 0, 6);
GLES20.glColorMask(true, true, true, true); // reset color masks for glDraw* calls ahead
```

Textures

Textures can be of two types—procedural textures and image textures. Procedural textures are generated on the fly, based on some algorithm, whereas image textures, as the name suggests, are textures loaded from image files, such as a .jpg, .png, and so on. This section demonstrates how to use image textures in ES 2.0.

> **Note**   Procedural and image textures are general classes of textures. In ES 2.0, however, textures are of two types—2D textures and cubemap textures.

Textures in OpenGL ES are 2D arrays of texture units known as *texels*. Similar to defining geometry for primitives (using the Cartesian coordinates x, y, and z), to apply texture(s) to a surface, specify the texture coordinates that correspond to the indices into this texture array data. Unlike the coordinates for geometry, texture coordinates use s and t (or u and v) as shown in Figure 5-2. Since texture coordinate space is normalized, both s and t range from 0 to 1. Please note that texture coordinates do not have units, so as to make them independent of the dimensions of source image or final rendered surface (composed of the texture).

> **Note** The process that applies a texture to some geometric object is called UV mapping.

To attach a 2D texture to a surface, we need to provide (s, t) coordinates from this texture such that it can cover the surface. If the specified coordinates (from texture) do not fit the surface completely, we can use texture wrap modes (provided by OpenGL ES) to help the textures wrap the surface, such as by repeating, mirroring, or clamping themselves. As a beginner, you may find it difficult to deal with all of these modes, so I shall only talk about the repeat wrap mode, defined as a static constant GL_REPEAT in the android.opengl.GLES20 class. Now, I shall demonstrate common uses of textures using ES 2.0.

> **Note** In OpenGL ES 2.0, textures can have non-power-of-two (*npot*) dimensions. However, the support for such textures is still limited to some devices. So, for all the applications in the source code in which we have demonstrated the use of textures, we have only used textures with power-of-two dimensions.

2D Texture

First, let's look at defining texture coordinates. Consider an example in which we wrap a texture around a square object. As shown in Figure 5-2, the bottom-left and top-right corners of the texture (image) are specified by (s, t) coordinates as (0, 0) and (1, 1), respectively. If the specified (s, t) coordinate is outside the range [0, 1], you can specify texture wrap mode, independently for both the s-coordinate and t-coordinate. Using wrap mode GL_REPEAT, texture outside this range is simply repeated.

Figure 5-2. Texture coordinate space: 64x64 texture

This square can be rendered using triangle primitives, as shown in Figure 5-3. Suppose we use glDrawElements to render it. The short array planeISA in Listing 5-4 consists of one of the ways to specify the indices, to access vertices from planeVFA vertex array (to render this square). To wrap texture around this square, when vertices are fetched using index array planeISA, texture coordinates must also be fetched. To make sure that texture coordinates are fetched in the same order as that of the vertices, you need to understand the sequence shown in Table 5-1.

Figure 5-3. Wrapping texture around a square object

Having read Table 5-1, you should understand how texture coordinates have to be mapped to vertex coordinates for a square object (or, in fact, any rectangular object). Now, there are two important things to note here:

- When passing texture coordinates to a vertex shader, you do not need to pass them separately for every primitive. Instead, pass them the way you pass vertices. In the context of this example, where you are wrapping a texture around a square object (or any rectangular object), define a texture coordinate array with four texture coordinates (Listing 5-4), instead of six (Table 5-1), similar to how you define a vertex coordinate array with four vertices, as shown in Listing 5-4.

Table 5-1. Wrapping Texture on a Square Object: Specifying Texture Coordinates

Position	Index	Vertex Coordinate	Texture Coordinate
top-right	2	(10, 10, 0)	(1, 1)
top-left	3	(-10, 10, 0)	(0, 1)
bottom-left	1	(-10, -10, 0)	(0, 0)
bottom-right	0	(10, -10, 0)	(1, 0)
top-right	2	(10, 10, 0)	(1, 1)
bottom-left	1	(-10, -10, 0)	(0, 0)

Listing 5-4. GL TEXTURE/src/com/apress/android/gltexture/GLES20Renderer.java

```
float[] planeVFA = {
  10.000000f,-10.000000f,0.000000f, // bottom-right
  -10.000000f,-10.000000f,0.000000f, // bottom-left
  10.000000f,10.000000f,0.000000f, // top-right
  -10.000000f,10.000000f,0.000000f, // top-left
};
```

```
float[] planeTFA = { // texture coordinate array
  // 1,0, 0,0, 1,1, 0,1
  1,1, 0,1, 1,0, 0,0
};

short[] planeISA = {
  2,3,1, // top-right, top-left, bottom-left
  0,2,1, // bottom-right, top-right, bottom-left
};
```

- Android uses the top-left corner as (0, 0) of the texture coordinate space, whereas OpenGL uses the bottom-left corner as (0, 0), which is why you must vertically flip the texture coordinates specified in the texture coordinate array. Therefore, (1, 0) becomes (1, 1), and (1, 1) becomes (1, 0), and so on.

Loading the Image Data

Using a texture in ES 2.0 first requires you to create a texture object. This texture object is represented by an unsigned integer (texture id), which is a reference to the texture object. The ES 2.0 function used to generate texture objects is called glGenTextures. In Android (SDK), it is accessed as the GLES20.glGenTextures method. This method has two overloaded versions. The one we use takes three arguments. In the first argument, specify the number of texture objects to be generated. Wrapping a single texture around a square only requires one texture object. The second argument is the array that will store the returned texture ids, referencing texture objects. To generate a single texture object, this array must be at least of size one, as shown in Listing 5-5 (int array textures). The last argument is the offset, and we will set this to "0".

Listing 5-5. GL TEXTURE/src/com/apress/android/gltexture/GLES20Renderer.java

```
int[] textures = new int[1];
GLES20.glGenTextures(1, textures, 0);
_textureId = textures[0];

GLES20.glBindTexture(GLES20.GL_TEXTURE_2D, _textureId);
InputStream is1 = _context.getResources().openRawResource(R.drawable.brick);
Bitmap img1;
try {
 img1 = BitmapFactory.decodeStream(is1);
} finally {
 try {
  is1.close();
 } catch(IOException e) {
  // e.printStackTrace();
 }
}
GLES20.glPixelStorei(GLES20.GL_UNPACK_ALIGNMENT, 1);
GLES20.glTexParameterf(GLES20.GL_TEXTURE_2D, GLES20.GL_TEXTURE_MIN_FILTER, GLES20.GL_NEAREST);
// or GL_LINEAR
GLES20.glTexParameterf(GLES20.GL_TEXTURE_2D, GLES20.GL_TEXTURE_MAG_FILTER, GLES20.GL_NEAREST);
// or GL_LINEAR
```

```
GLES20.glTexParameteri(GLES20.GL_TEXTURE_2D, GLES20.GL_TEXTURE_WRAP_S, GLES20.GL_REPEAT);
GLES20.glTexParameteri(GLES20.GL_TEXTURE_2D, GLES20.GL_TEXTURE_WRAP_T, GLES20.GL_REPEAT);
GLUtils.texImage2D(GLES20.GL_TEXTURE_2D, 0, img1, 0);
```

As ES 2.0 supports two types of textures (that is, 2D textures and cubemap textures), when you have generated a texture object, you must bind its corresponding id to any of these types (that is, 2D texture or cubemap texture).

This is done by calling the method GLES20.glBindTexture. This method takes two arguments. The first argument is the texture type, defined as constants—GLES20.GL_TEXTURE_2D and GLES20.GL_TEXTURE_CUBE_MAP. The second argument is the texture id corresponding to a texture object.

Finally, after generating a texture object and binding it, load the image data. To do so, call the method GLUtils.texImage2D. This method has three overloaded versions. The one we use takes four arguments—int type, int level, Bitmap bitmap, and int border. The type argument specifies the texture type. The level argument specifies the mipmap level to load; set this to "0", which means mipmap level "0".

Note Textures have *minification* and *magnification* filtering modes associated with them (when the size of the projected primitive on the screen is smaller than the size of the texture, *minification* is caused, whereas when the size of the projected primitive on the screen is larger than the size of the texture, *magnification* is caused). When the minification and magnification filters are set to GL_NEAREST, the specified texture coordinate is used to fetch a single *texel* (*texel* nearest to the specified texture coordinate) from the texture. This is known as nearest sampling. When the minification and magnification filters are set to GL_LINEAR, the specified texture coordinate is used to fetch a bilinear sample (average of four *texels*) from the texture about the texture coordinate.

Nearest sampling can produce visual artifacts when a texture is wrapped (around a surface) by the interpolation of texture coordinates from one vertex to another. Mipmapping is the solution to avoid this artifact.

The idea behind mipmapping is to build a chain of images known as a mipmap chain. The mipmap chain begins with the originally specified image (mipmap level "0"), then continues with each subsequent image being one-half as large in each dimension as the one before it. This chain continues until we reach a single 1 x 1 texture at the bottom of the chain.

To learn more about such advanced OpenGL ES 2.0 concepts, read OpenGL®ES 2.0 Programming Guide by Aaftab Munshi, Dan Ginsburg and Dave Shreiner (Addison-Wesley, 2008), from which this quotation is taken.

The third argument is the Bitmap resource, which has to be decoded for use (as shown in Listing 5-5). In the last argument, you must specify the border. For most cases, this is set as "0", meaning "no-border."

In Listing 5-5, the code snippet used between the calls to GLES20.glBindTexture and GLUtils.texImage2D is used to fetch the image resource, which is used as a texture, and set the texture parameters. You must understand the use of the following call—glTexParameteri(GLES20.GL_TEXTURE_2D,

GLES20.GL_TEXTURE_WRAP_S, GLES20.GL_REPEAT). This sets the repeat wrap mode for the s-coordinate of texture. The call to glTexParameterf(GLES20.GL_TEXTURE_2D, GLES20.GL_TEXTURE_MIN_FILTER, GLES20.GL_NEAREST) sets the minification filter to GL_NEAREST. To try the two filtering modes in a real application, modify the Renderer class in the *GL TEXTURE* application to reflect these changes. You can load this application into your Eclipse workspace by importing the archive file Chapter5/gltexture.zip.

In the Renderer class of this application, set the GL_TEXTURE_MIN_FILTER and GL_TEXTURE_MAG_FILTER - each of these modes, to use GL_LINEAR filter. The output, after making this change, is similar to Figure 5-4, but the texture will be hazy because of bilinear sampling caused by the use of GL_LINEAR filter. The following line of code—GLES20.glPixelStorei(GLES20.GL_UNPACK_ALIGNMENT, 1)—in Listing 5-5 is used to specify the byte boundary for the rows of pixel (image) data.

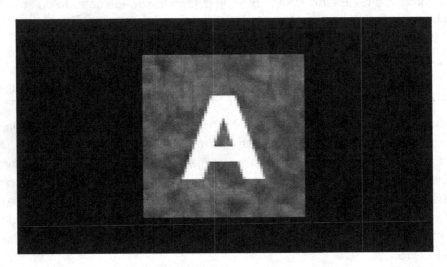

Figure 5-4. Using single texture with an object

sampler2D Uniform Variable

Now, take a look at the *shader* code for texturing. The vertex–fragment shader pair in Listing 5-6 demonstrates the basics of how 2D texturing is done in a *shader*.

Listing 5-6. GL TEXTURE/src/com/apress/android/gltexture/GLES20Renderer.java

```
private final String _planeVertexShaderCode =
  "attribute vec4 aPosition; \n"
+ "attribute vec2 aCoord; \n"
+ "varying vec2 vCoord; \n"
+ "uniform mat4 uMVP; \n"
+ "void main() { \n"
+ " gl_Position = uMVP * aPosition; \n"
+ " vCoord = aCoord; \n"
+ "} \n";

private final String _planeFragmentShaderCode =
  "#ifdef GL_FRAGMENT_PRECISION_HIGH \n"
```

```
+ "precision highp float; \n"
+ "#else \n"
+ "precision mediump float; \n"
+ "#endif \n"
+ "varying vec2 vCoord; \n"
+ "uniform sampler2D uSampler; \n"
+ "void main() { \n"
+ " gl_FragColor = texture2D(uSampler,vCoord); \n"
+ "} \n";
```

The attribute variable aCoord (of type vec2) in the vertex shader receives the texture coordinate (Listing 5-4) and passes it to the fragment shader as a varying variable vCoord (of type vec2). The fragment shader uses this varying variable to get the interpolated texture coordinates for fetching the texture units (*texels*) from the loaded texture.

The uniform variable uSampler in the fragment shader (Listing 5-6) is of type sampler2D. Variables of type sampler* (sampler2D and samplerCube) are special types of a uniform variable, used to fetch from a texture map. The sampler* uniform has to be loaded with a value specifying the number of current texture (in a zero-based manner).

Note   sampler2D uniform is used with 2D textures, and samplerCube uniform is used with cubemap textures.

This value is loaded using the glActiveTexture function. If a single texture is used, this function takes constant GL_TEXTURE0 as argument, as shown in Listing 5-7. For every successive texture used, the next higher constant is used.

Listing 5-7. GL TEXTURE/src/com/apress/android/gltexture/GLES20Renderer.java

```
GLES20.glUseProgram(_planeProgram);

GLES20.glActiveTexture(GLES20.GL_TEXTURE0);
GLES20.glBindTexture(GLES20.GL_TEXTURE_2D, _textureId);
GLES20.glUniform1i(_planeUSamplerLocation, 0);

GLES20.glUniformMatrix4fv(_planeUMVPLocation, 1, false, _MVPMatrix, 0);
GLES20.glVertexAttribPointer(_planeAPositionLocation, 3, GLES20.GL_FLOAT, false, 12, _planeVFB);
GLES20.glEnableVertexAttribArray(_planeAPositionLocation);
GLES20.glVertexAttribPointer(_planeACoordinateLocation, 2, GLES20.GL_FLOAT, false, 8, _planeTFB);
GLES20.glEnableVertexAttribArray(_planeACoordinateLocation);
GLES20.glDrawElements(GLES20.GL_TRIANGLES, 6, GLES20.GL_UNSIGNED_SHORT, _planeISB);
```

The subsequent call to glBindTexture binds the active texture to its texture type. Finally, to make this texture ready for use with the *shader program*, call glUniform1i and pass it the sampler location as an argument, and an additional argument specifying the number of current texture (in a zero-based manner). So, for the first texture used, this value is "0".

The built-in function texture2D in the fragment shader (Listing 5-6) is used to fetch from the texture map. It takes the sampler2D uniform and vec2 texture coordinate as arguments. This function returns a vec4, representing the color fetched from the texture map. If the format of the texture is RGB, then the vec4 returned is (R, G, B, 1.0). If this format is RGBA, then the vec4 returned is (R, G, B, A).

Using Texture and Color

Along with the color (vec4) fetched from the texture map, we can also use additional colors (Figure 5-5) with the rendered object. Inside the fragment shader, you can create a color represented as a variable of type vec4. Then, you can add this color to the texture color.

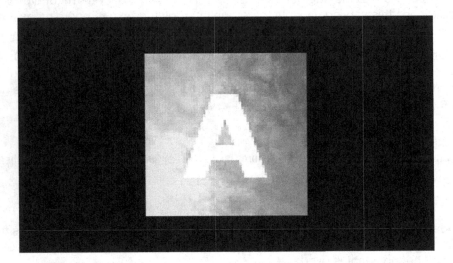

Figure 5-5. *Using texture and color*

By now you should understand that you can either create a color directly inside the fragment shader or you can use an attribute variable in the vertex shader to receive colors separately for each vertex and pass this per-vertex color (as a varying variable) to the fragment shader. Listing 5-8 contains the vertex and fragment shader code required to set the fragment color as a combination of texture color and varying color.

Listing 5-8. *GL TEXTURE COLOR/src/com/apress/android/gltexturecolor/GLES20Renderer.java*

```
private final String _planeVertexShaderCode =
  "attribute vec4 aPosition; \n"
+ "attribute vec2 aCoord; \n"
+ "attribute vec4 aColor; \n"
+ "varying vec2 vCoord; \n"
+ "varying vec4 vColor; \n"
+ "uniform mat4 uMVP; \n"
+ "void main() { \n"
+ " gl_Position = uMVP * aPosition; \n"
+ " vCoord = aCoord; \n"
+ " vColor = aColor; \n"
+ "} \n";
```

```
private final String _planeFragmentShaderCode =
  "#ifdef GL_FRAGMENT_PRECISION_HIGH \n"
+ "precision highp float; \n"
+ "#else \n"
+ "precision mediump float; \n"
+ "#endif \n"
+ "varying vec2 vCoord; \n"
+ "varying vec4 vColor; \n"
+ "uniform sampler2D uSampler; \n"
+ "void main() { \n"
+ " vec4 textureColor; \n"
+ " textureColor = texture2D(uSampler,vCoord); \n"
+ " gl_FragColor = vColor + textureColor; \n"
+ "} \n";
```

Cubemap Textures

Cubemap textures are another type of texture in ES 2.0. They are called cubemap textures, because a cubemap texture is composed of six 2D textures in which each texture represents one of the six faces of a cube.

Texels from a cubemap texture are fetched in a complex way, compared to how they are fetched from a 2D texture. However, defining a texture coordinate array for a cubemap texture is a lot easier than doing so for a 2D texture.

Listing 5-9 contains array definitions from the *GL CUBEMAP TEXTURE* application (the output is seen in Figure 3-5) from the source code for this chapter (Chapter5/glcubemaptexture.zip). This application demonstrates using a cubemap texture.

As indicated in Listing 5-9, cubeVFA is the vertex coordinate array, cubeISA is the index array, and cubeTFA is the texture coordinate array. Arrays cubeVFA and cubeTFA are similar, except that the texture coordinates in cubeTFA are filled with ones. Compared to the (s, t) coordinates used in 2D textures, cubemap textures use an additional coordinate, because fetching *texels* from a cubemap texture requires 3D vectors. Please note that we do not have to worry about the underlying process that does so. Fetching *texels* automatically takes place using the built-in ES 2.0 function textureCube, called inside the fragment shader.

Listing 5-9. GL CUBEMAP TEXTURE/src/com/apress/android/glcubemaptexture/GLES20Renderer.java

```
float[] cubeVFA = { // vertex (float) coordinate array
  -0.5f,-0.5f,0.5f,   0.5f,-0.5f,0.5f,   0.5f,0.5f,0.5f,   -0.5f,0.5f,0.5f,
  -0.5f,-0.5f,-0.5f,  0.5f,-0.5f,-0.5f,  0.5f,0.5f,-0.5f,  -0.5f,0.5f,-0.5f
};

short[] cubeISA = { // index (short) array
  0,4,5,  0,1,5,  5,6,2,  5,1,2,
  5,6,7,  5,4,7,  7,6,2,  7,3,2,
  7,3,0,  7,4,0,  0,3,2,  0,1,2
};
```

```
float[] cubeTFA = { // texture (float) coordinate array
  -1,-1,1,   1,-1,1,   1,1,1,   -1,1,1,
  -1,-1,-1,  1,-1,-1,  1,1,-1,  -1,1,-1
};
```

Loading Images for a Cubemap Texture

Similar to 2D textures (Listing 5-5), when you generate a texture object for a cubemap texture, you need to bind its corresponding id to the texture type. For a cubemap texture, this is done by GLES20.glBindTexture(GLES20.GL_TEXTURE_CUBE_MAP, _textureId);.

Similarly, to set the texture parameters for using a cubemap texture, the first argument passed to the GLES20.glTexParameteri method should be GLES20.GL_TEXTURE_CUBE_MAP.

Because a cubemap texture has six faces, instead of a single call to the GLUtils.texImage2D method, you need to call this method six times, corresponding to each face. To do so, pass the first argument as a constant (Listing 5-10) specifying the face:

- GLES20.GL_TEXTURE_CUBE_MAP_POSITIVE_X

- GLES20.GL_TEXTURE_CUBE_MAP_NEGATIVE_X

- GLES20.GL_TEXTURE_CUBE_MAP_POSITIVE_Y

- GLES20.GL_TEXTURE_CUBE_MAP_NEGATIVE_Y

- GLES20.GL_TEXTURE_CUBE_MAP_POSITIVE_Z

- GLES20.GL_TEXTURE_CUBE_MAP_NEGATIVE_Z

For the *GL CUBEMAP TEXTURE* application, I have used six different textures. So six different Bitmap resources are used, two of which are shown in Listing 5-10.

Listing 5-10. GL CUBEMAP TEXTURE/src/com/apress/android/glcubemaptexture/GLES20Renderer.java

```
InputStream is1 = _context.getResources().openRawResource(R.drawable.brick1);
Bitmap img1;
try {
 img1 = BitmapFactory.decodeStream(is1);
} finally {
 try {
  is1.close();
 } catch(IOException e) {
  // e.printStackTrace();
 }
}
GLUtils.texImage2D(GLES20.GL_TEXTURE_CUBE_MAP_POSITIVE_X, 0, img1, 0);
InputStream is2 = _context.getResources().openRawResource(R.drawable.brick2);
Bitmap img2;
try {
 img2 = BitmapFactory.decodeStream(is2);
} finally {
```

```
try {
 is2.close();
} catch(IOException e) {
 // e.printStackTrace();
 }
}
GLUtils.texImage2D(GLES20.GL_TEXTURE_CUBE_MAP_NEGATIVE_X, 0, img2, 0);
```

samplerCube Uniform Variable

The fragment shader code for a cubemap texture uses samplerCube uniform in place of sampler2D (Listing 5-6) uniform. Listing 5-11 shows the fragment shader code from the *GL CUBEMAP TEXTURE* application. It uses the built-in function textureCube to fetch from the cubemap texture. This function is almost identical to the texture2D function. The only difference is that the texture coordinate is a vec3, instead of vec2 and the sampler* type must be samplerCube.

Listing 5-11. GL CUBEMAP TEXTURE/src/com/apress/android/glcubemaptexture/GLES20Renderer.java

```
private final String _cubeFragmentShaderCode =
  "#ifdef GL_FRAGMENT_PRECISION_HIGH \n"
 + "precision highp float; \n"
 + "#else \n"
 + "precision mediump float; \n"
 + "#endif \n"
 + "varying vec3 vCoord; \n"
 + "uniform samplerCube uSampler; \n"
 + "void main() { \n"
 + " gl_FragColor = textureCube(uSampler,vCoord); \n"
 + "} \n";
```

Multi-Texturing

You can also extend the *GL TEXTURE* application to use more than one texture for the rendered object. Use of two textures (Figure 5-6) with the rendered object is demonstrated in the *GL MULTI TEXTURE* application (Chapter5/glmultitexture.zip) with output as seen in Figure 5-7.

 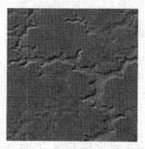

Figure 5-6. Textures from GIMP

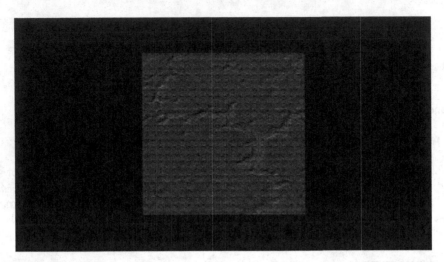

Figure 5-7. GL MULTI TEXTURE application

The two textures used in this application have identical dimensions. For this reason, the same texture coordinate array is used to fetch *texels* from both these textures. As you may have guessed, using two 2D textures with the rendered object does require two separate `sampler2D` uniforms. Listing 5-12 contains the vertex-fragment shader pair from this application.

Listing 5-12. GL MULTI TEXTURE/src/com/apress/android/glmultitexture/GLES20Renderer.java

```
private final String _planeVertexShaderCode =
  "attribute vec4 aPosition; \n"
 + "attribute vec2 aCoord; \n"
 + "varying vec2 vCoord; \n"
 + "uniform mat4 uMVP; \n"
 + "void main() { \n"
 + " gl_Position = uMVP * aPosition; \n"
 + " vCoord = aCoord; \n"
 + "} \n";

private final String _planeFragmentShaderCode =
  "#ifdef GL_FRAGMENT_PRECISION_HIGH \n"
 + "precision highp float; \n"
 + "#else \n"
 + "precision mediump float; \n"
 + "#endif \n"
 + "varying vec2 vCoord; \n"
 + "uniform sampler2D uSampler1; \n"
 + "uniform sampler2D uSampler2; \n"
 + "void main() { \n"
 + " vec4 textureColor1,textureColor2; \n"
 + " textureColor1 = texture2D(uSampler1,vCoord); \n"
 + " textureColor2 = texture2D(uSampler2,vCoord); \n"
 + " gl_FragColor = textureColor1 * textureColor2; \n"
 + "} \n";
```

Because the texture2D function returns a vec4 texture color, there is no restriction as to how you combine the texture colors. You can perform any operation between the texture colors, and finally set the resultant color as the fragment color. As shown in Listing 5-12, texture colors textureColor1 and textureColor2 are multiplied, and the resultant color is set as the fragment color:

```
gl_FragColor = textureColor1 * textureColor2;
```

When using multiple 2D textures, you must generate texture objects for each texture to be used. Please note that, although a cubemap texture uses six 2D textures, a cubemap texture is a separate type of texture in ES 2.0, which explains why it only requires a single texture object.

So, to use two 2D textures, two texture objects must be generated, as shown in Listing 5-13. Each of the texture ids must be bound to the texture type, which, in this case, is GL_TEXTURE_2D. Similarly, other ES 2.0 functions to successfully load the image data—glPixelStorei, glTexParameter* and texImage2D—must be separately called for each texture object, regardless of the number of Bitmap resources used (Listing 5-13).

Listing 5-13. GL MULTI TEXTURE/src/com/apress/android/glmultitexture/GLES20Renderer.java

```
int[] textures = new int[2];
GLES20.glGenTextures(2, textures, 0);
_textureId1 = textures[0];
_textureId2 = textures[1];

// load the 1st texture

GLES20.glBindTexture(GLES20.GL_TEXTURE_2D, _textureId1);
InputStream is1 = _context.getResources().openRawResource(R.drawable.brick1);
Bitmap img1;
try {
 img1 = BitmapFactory.decodeStream(is1);
} finally {
 try {
  is1.close();
 } catch(IOException e) {
  // e.printStackTrace();
 }
}
GLES20.glPixelStorei(GLES20.GL_UNPACK_ALIGNMENT, 1);
GLES20.glTexParameterf(GLES20.GL_TEXTURE_2D, GLES20.GL_TEXTURE_MIN_FILTER, GLES20.GL_NEAREST);
// GL_LINEAR
GLES20.glTexParameterf(GLES20.GL_TEXTURE_2D, GLES20.GL_TEXTURE_MAG_FILTER, GLES20.GL_NEAREST);
GLES20.glTexParameteri(GLES20.GL_TEXTURE_2D, GLES20.GL_TEXTURE_WRAP_S, GLES20.GL_REPEAT);
GLES20.glTexParameteri(GLES20.GL_TEXTURE_2D, GLES20.GL_TEXTURE_WRAP_T, GLES20.GL_REPEAT);
GLUtils.texImage2D(GLES20.GL_TEXTURE_2D, 0, img1, 0);

// load the 2nd texture

GLES20.glBindTexture(GLES20.GL_TEXTURE_2D, _textureId2);
InputStream is2 = _context.getResources().openRawResource(R.drawable.brick2);
Bitmap img2;
```

```
try {
 img2 = BitmapFactory.decodeStream(is2);
} finally {
 try {
  is2.close();
 } catch(IOException e) {
  // e.printStackTrace();
 }
}
GLES20.glPixelStorei(GLES20.GL_UNPACK_ALIGNMENT, 1);
GLES20.glTexParameterf(GLES20.GL_TEXTURE_2D, GLES20.GL_TEXTURE_MIN_FILTER, GLES20.GL_NEAREST);
// GL_LINEAR
GLES20.glTexParameterf(GLES20.GL_TEXTURE_2D, GLES20.GL_TEXTURE_MAG_FILTER, GLES20.GL_NEAREST);
GLES20.glTexParameteri(GLES20.GL_TEXTURE_2D, GLES20.GL_TEXTURE_WRAP_S, GLES20.GL_REPEAT);
GLES20.glTexParameteri(GLES20.GL_TEXTURE_2D, GLES20.GL_TEXTURE_WRAP_T, GLES20.GL_REPEAT);
GLUtils.texImage2D(GLES20.GL_TEXTURE_2D, 0, img2, 0);
```

Lighting Effects Using Shader Programs

OpenGL ES 1.1 provides built-in lighting models to compute the lighting equations for various types of light source (point light, spot light, and so on). However, in ES 2.0, you must do all the math necessary to perform lighting effects. For this, you must know about lighting and shading. Lighting (*physics* terminology) is the interaction between a surface (made up of a specific material) and a light source. Shading is a technique in computer-graphics that uses lighting to determine the final color of a fragment.

Illumination Models

A model for the interaction of light with a surface is called an illumination model (also known as a lighting model). In computer-graphics, the commonly used illumination models are *Lambert* and *Phong*. In the *Lambert* model, the reflection of light from an object's surface is independent of the viewing direction (that is, the vector pointing from the viewer to the object's surface). In contrast, in the *Phong* model, the reflection of light depends on the viewing direction. This section focuses on the *Lambert* model.

> **Note**   The type of reflection in the *Lambert* model is known as *diffuse reflection*. Diffuse reflections from the surfaces are scattered with equal intensity in all directions, independent of the viewing direction. Surfaces that behave this way are called *Lambertian reflectors*.

To implement this model, you must understand *Lambert's Cosine Law*. This states that *the reflection of light from a Lambertian reflector varies as the cosine of the angle between the normal to the surface and the direction of the reflected ray.*

For this reason, a surface perpendicular to the direction of the incident light appears brighter than a surface that is oblique to the direction of this light. Next, we talk about the lighting equations involved in this model.

Diffuse Reflection: Equations for Illumination

Diffuse reflection involves two vectors—the vector *S* from surface to light source, and the normal *N* to surface, as shown in Figure 5-8. For obvious reasons, when light arrives along *N*, the illumination of the surface is highest. It is zero, when light is perpendicular to *N*.

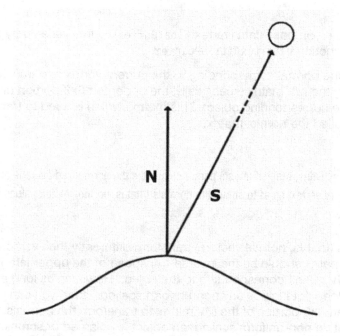

Figure 5-8. Diffuse reflection: the circle represents the point light source

Note   Although we are talking about a surface, in the context of an ES 2.0 application, this surface is a triangle primitive represented as a set of vertices. So, in this context, the surface does not explicitly interact with the incoming light; however, the vertices do.

If θ is the angle between *N* and *S*, then, apart from the two cases mentioned, for all other cases the illumination will be proportional to cos(θ). Therefore, the amount of radiation striking the surface is *lin*(*N.S*), where *lin* is the intensity of the light source and *(N.S)* is the dot product of vectors *N* and *S*. Because only a fraction of the incoming light is actually scattered, you need to introduce a coefficient into this equation, so that you can determine the intensity of the outgoing light:

Iout = K(lin(N.S))

Here, K is the reflection coefficient, which represents the fraction of the incoming light that is scattered. *Iout* is the intensity of the outgoing light. Now, we describe the shading technique in which, using this lighting equation, we evaluate *Iout* at each vertex of an object (specifically, the primitives constituting this object).

Lighting Equation in Vertex Shader

To implement this lighting equation using a *shader program*:

- Inside the vertex shader, store the current vertex (say, in a variable vertex of type vec4).

    - Recall that you pass data (vertex FloatBuffer) to this variable by calling the ES 2.0 function glVertexAttribPointer.

- Next, store the normal corresponding to the current vertex and transform this normal using the *MV* matrix (specifically, the upper-left 3x3 portion of the *MV* matrix) of the corresponding object. This matrix, which is used to transform the normal, is called the normal matrix.

> **Note**   As Chapter 4 explains, the Perl (mesh) parser calculates the normalized average of adjacent mesh-normals for every vertex, so as to obtain the normals (that is, normal vectors) along them.

- Normals (that is, normal vectors) transform differently than vertices. The normal matrix should be the inverse-transpose of the upper-left 3x3 portion of the *MV* matrix corresponding to the object. However, as long as the *MV* matrix does not include any non-uniform scalings, then you can use the upper-left 3x3 portion of the *MV* matrix to transform the normals. Please note that, in non-uniform scaling, an object is enlarged or shrunk by a factor that is not the same along all axes.

> **Note**   To look deeper into the concepts on non-uniform scaling of normals, refer the following URL: http://www.lighthouse3d.com/tutorials/glsl-tutorial/the-normal-matrix/.

- Inside the vertex shader, store the current (transformed) normal in a variable of type vec3 using the following code. This normal corresponds to the *N* vector, shown in Figure 5-8.

    ```
    vec3 normal = normalize(vec3(uNormal * aNormal));
    ```

■ Here, uNormal is the uniform variable (of type mat3) to store the normal matrix, and aNormal is an attribute variable that receives vertex normals. Similar to how we pass vertices using glVertexAttribPointer, we also pass the vertex normals. Recall from Chapter 4 ("Parsing Objects for OpenGL ES") that you can access the vertex normals from the "normal:" block in the parser's output text file.

■ The normalize function, as the name suggests, is a built-in function in ES 2.0 that helps normalize the given vector. Normalization is necessary to avoid any scaling of the vectors.

■ To pass the 3x3 normal matrix to the vertex shader, use the ES 2.0 function glUniformMatrix3fv, and call it as: GLES20.glUniformMatrix3fv (_tankUNormalLocation, 1, false, _tankNormalMatrix, 0);

■ Here, _tankNormalMatrix (float[9]) is the normal matrix, obtained by copying the upper-left 3x3 portion of the *MV* matrix corresponding to the object (Listing 5-14). You do not need to create a separate *MV* matrix to copy the required values; instead, copy the values from the *MVP* matrix, before it is combined with the projection transformation, as shown in the following code.

Listing 5-14. VERTEX POINT LIGHTING/src/com/apress/android/vertexpointlighting/GLES20Renderer.java

```
_tankNormalMatrix[0] = _tankMVPMatrix[0];
_tankNormalMatrix[1] = _tankMVPMatrix[1];
_tankNormalMatrix[2] = _tankMVPMatrix[2]; // from 1st column, ending at [3]

_tankNormalMatrix[3] = _tankMVPMatrix[4];
_tankNormalMatrix[4] = _tankMVPMatrix[5];
_tankNormalMatrix[5] = _tankMVPMatrix[6]; // from 2nd column, ending at [7]

_tankNormalMatrix[6] = _tankMVPMatrix[8];
_tankNormalMatrix[7] = _tankMVPMatrix[9];
_tankNormalMatrix[8] = _tankMVPMatrix[10]; // from 3rd column, ending at [11]

System.arraycopy(_tankMVPMatrix, 0, _tankMVMatrix, 0, 16);
Matrix.multiplyMM(_tankMVPMatrix, 0, _ProjectionMatrix, 0, _tankMVMatrix, 0);
```

■ Next, to obtain the *S* vector for the current vertex, take its difference with the light source position.

■ For this, store the light source position in a global variable, inside the vertex shader (Listing 5-16). This variable is usually declared as a constant variable, by using the const keyword:

```
const vec4 lightPositionWorld = vec4(10.0, 10.0, 0.0, 1.0);
```

■ As we are dealing with a point light source, we just need a single vertex to represent it, irrespective of the shape of the light source. If you have modeled this light source object in Blender, you can obtain its center by reading the global median value from the *properties shelf*, as shown in Figure 5-9.

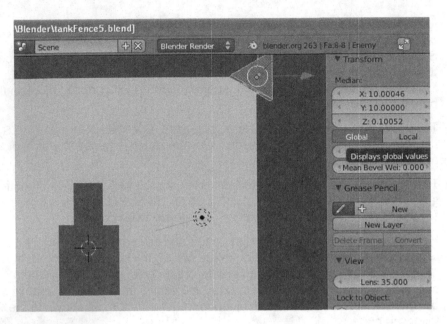

Figure 5-9. Blender: obtaining the center of object

> **Note**   In the source code for this chapter, inside the Blender folder, you will find Blender files named
> `pointLight*`. You can open these files to see how you can add a point light source. Instead of using
> a sphere as a light source object, I have used an Icosphere mesh, which can be easily added using the
> Add menu (from the *Info* window). I have used this object in both *VERTEX POINT LIGHTING* and
> *FRAGMENT POINT LIGHTING* applications.In these applications, I have demonstrated lighting/shading
> effects using a point light source. This application contains the Tank and Light objects, where the Light object
> is an Icosphere added from Blender.

- ■   Because the normal vector (***N***) is in eye-space (to get points and vectors in
  eye-space, they must be transformed using their respective *MV* matrices),
  you must also transform the ***S*** vector into eye-space, so it becomes
  possible to take their dot product. For this, make sure the current vertex
  position and the light source position are transformed using their respective
  MV matrices. In most graphical applications, the light source is usually
  fixed. However in the application I have provided for demonstrating
  lighting/shading effects, I have made it optional to rotate the light source
  (Listing 5-15). The vertex shader code in Listing 5-16 consists of a uniform
  variable uMVLight to store the *MV* matrix _pointMVMatrix for the light
  source.

Listing 5-15. VERTEX POINT LIGHTING/src/com/apress/android/vertexpointlighting/GLES20Renderer.java

```
if(!_rotatePointOnly) {
 Matrix.setIdentityM(_tankRMatrix, 0);
 Matrix.rotateM(_tankRMatrix, 0, _zAngle, 0, 0, 1);
}
Matrix.multiplyMM(_tankMVPMatrix, 0, _ViewMatrix, 0, _tankRMatrix, 0);
if(_rotatePointOnly) {
 Matrix.rotateM(_pointRMatrix, 0, _zAngle * 0.5f, 0, 0, 1);
 Matrix.multiplyMM(_pointMVMatrix, 0, _ViewMatrix, 0, _pointRMatrix, 0);
 Matrix.multiplyMM(_pointMVPMatrix, 0, _ProjectionMatrix, 0, _pointMVMatrix, 0);
}
```

■ The uniform variable uMV inside the vertex shader stores the *MV* matrix for the object. This matrix is obtained by copying the entire *MVP* matrix before the *MVP* matrix is combined with projection transformation. As shown in Listing 5-14, the System.arraycopy method is used to copy the *MVP* matrix to *MV* matrix for the object. You need this *MV* matrix to transform the vertex positions into eye-space.

Listing 5-16. VERTEX POINT LIGHTING/src/com/apress/android/vertexpointlighting/GLES20Renderer.java

```
private final String _tankVertexShaderCode =
  "attribute vec3 aPosition; \n"
 + "attribute vec3 aNormal; \n"
 + "varying float diffuseIntensity; \n"
 + "uniform mat3 uNormal; \n"
 + "uniform mat4 uMV; \n"
 + "uniform mat4 uMVP; \n"
 + "uniform mat4 uMVLight; \n"
 + "const vec4 lightPositionWorld = vec4(10.0, 10.0, 0.0, 1.0); \n"
 + "void main() { \n"
 + " vec4 vertex = vec4(aPosition[0], aPosition[1], aPosition[2], 1.0); \n"
 + " \n"
 + " vec3 normal = normalize(vec3(uNormal * aNormal)); \n"
 + " // vec3 normal = vec3(uNormal * aNormal); \n"
 + " vec4 vertexEye = vec4(uMV * vertex); \n"
 + " vec4 lightPositionEye = vec4(uMVLight * lightPositionWorld); \n"
 + " vec3 ds = normalize(vec3(lightPositionEye - vertexEye)); \n"
 + " // vec3 ds = vec3(lightPositionEye - vertexEye); \n"
 + " \n"
 + " // diffuseIntensity = Ld * Kd * max(dot(ds, normal), ambientIntensity); \n"
 + " diffuseIntensity = max(dot(ds, normal), 0.210); \n"
 + " diffuseIntensity = 0.570 * 0.210 * diffuseIntensity; \n"
 + " \n"
 + " gl_Position = vec4(uMVP * vertex); // ensures that we provide a vec4 \n"
 + "} \n";
```

■ Finally, obtain the *S* vector for the current vertex by taking its difference with the light source position. The variable ds (Listing 5-16) stores this difference.

- To determine the intensity of outgoing light (*Iout*) at the current vertex, take the dot product of ds and normal vectors, using the built-in function dot(vec*, vec*).

  - The vertex shader code in Listing 5-16 uses the built-in function max(float, float) to make sure that ambient light is also taken into account.

  - Ambient light sets a general level of brightness for the object. It is a background light, and its intensity is constant for all the objects in the scene, for all the surfaces, and over all directions.

  - Using the max function, the brighter among ambient ("0.210") and diffuse light, is selected as the diffuseIntensity.

  - As discussed, to obtain the final intensity of outgoing light, multiply the diffuseIntensity variable with the reflection coefficient (also set as "0.210"), as well as the intensity of incoming light (Listing 5-16).

Finally, the diffuseIntensity varying variable is passed to the fragment shader and is set as the fragment color, as shown in Listing 5-17. Please note that the diffuse intensity can also be combined with the material color for the object.

Listing 5-17. VERTEX POINT LIGHTING/src/com/apress/android/vertexpointlighting/GLES20Renderer.java

```
private final String _tankFragmentShaderCode =
  "precision lowp float; // not to be done in a vertex shader \n"
+ "varying float diffuseIntensity; \n"
+ "void main() { \n"
+ " vec3 diffuse = vec3(diffuseIntensity); \n"
+ " // gl_FragColor = vec4(0.1, 0.1, 0.25, 1.0) + vec4(diffuse, 1.0); \n"
+ " gl_FragColor = vec4(diffuse, 1.0); \n"
+ "} \n";
```

Because you are interpolating the final intensity of light (Figure 5-10), shading effect will be more pronounced, as shown in Figure 5-11 (output of *VERTEX POINT LIGHTING* application from the source code), which can lead to unrealistic effects on some occasions.

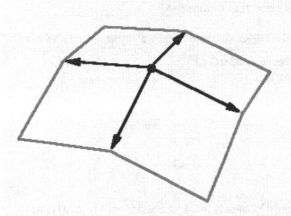

Figure 5-10. *Unwrapped faces around a vertex*

Figure 5-11. *Interpolation of lighting (shade)*

Interpolating Vertex Normal

To make the shading effects more realistic, instead of interpolating diffuse intensity, you can interpolate vertex normal across fragments. To demonstrate this, I have created an application - *FRAGMENT POINT LIGHTING*. Load this application into your Eclipse workspace by importing the archive file Chapter5/fragmentpointlighting.zip.

As shown in Listing 5-18, in place of the vertex shader, the fragment shader is now implementing the lighting equation. The normal for current vertex is transformed into eye-space in the vertex shader, and, because it is of type varying, it gets interpolated across the fragments. This leads to more realistic shading effects, as shown in Figure 5-12.

Listing 5-18. FRAGMENT POINT LIGHTING/src/com/apress/android/fragmentpointlighting/GLES20Renderer.java

```
private final String _tankVertexShaderCode =
  "attribute vec3 aPosition; \n"
+ "attribute vec3 aNormal; \n"
+ "varying vec4 vertex; \n"
+ "varying vec3 normal; \n"
+ "uniform mat3 uNormal; \n"
+ "uniform mat4 uMV; \n"
+ "uniform mat4 uMVP; \n"
+ "uniform mat4 uMVLight; \n"
+ "void main() { \n"
+ " vertex = vec4(aPosition[0], aPosition[1], aPosition[2], 1.0); \n"
+ " normal = normalize(vec3(uNormal * aNormal)); \n"
+ "  \n"
+ " gl_Position = vec4(uMVP * vertex); // ensures that we provide a vec4 \n"
+ "} \n";


private final String _tankFragmentShaderCode =
  "#ifdef GL_FRAGMENT_PRECISION_HIGH \n"
+ "precision highp float; \n"
+ "#else \n"
+ "precision mediump float; \n"
+ "#endif \n"
+ "varying float diffuseIntensity; \n"
+ "varying vec4 vertex; \n"
+ "varying vec3 normal; \n"
+ "uniform mat3 uNormal; \n"
+ "uniform mat4 uMV; \n"
+ "uniform mat4 uMVP; \n"
+ "uniform mat4 uMVLight; \n"
+ "const vec4 lightPositionWorld = vec4(10.0, 10.0, 0.0, 1.0); \n"
+ "void main() { \n"
+ " float diffuseIntensity; \n"
+ " vec4 vertexEye = vec4(uMV * vertex); \n"
+ " vec4 lightPositionEye = vec4(uMVLight * lightPositionWorld); \n"
+ " vec3 ds = normalize(vec3(lightPositionEye - vertexEye)); \n"
+ "  \n"
+ " diffuseIntensity = max(dot(ds, normal), 0.210); \n"
+ " diffuseIntensity = 0.570 * 0.210 * diffuseIntensity; \n"
+ " vec3 diffuse = vec3(diffuseIntensity); \n"
+ " // vec4 materialColor = vec4(0.1, 0.1, 0.25, 1.0); \n"
+ " // gl_FragColor = vec4(0.1, 0.1, 0.25, 1.0) + vec4(diffuse, 1.0); \n"
+ " gl_FragColor = vec4(diffuse, 1.0); \n"
+ "} \n";
```

Figure 5-12. Realistic lighting effects by interpolating normals

Summary

At the start of this chapter, I explained various ways to use textures with the rendered object. I discussed using:

- single texture
- combination of textures
- combination of texture and color
- cubemap texture

Then, I talked about the *Lambert* illumination model and how to implement it using *shader programs*.

In the next chapter, we will continue the development of our *Tank Fence* game, where I will introduce two new classes to help us deal with Missile and Enemy game objects.

6

Taking the Development Ahead

In this chapter, we will continue the development of our *Tank Fence* game. For this, we will be using the *TANK FENCE 3* application from the previous chapter. First, you have to make small changes to the UI of this application. Then, I will introduce two new classes to help us deal with Missile and Enemy game objects.

Specifying the Render Mode

In some graphical applications, rendering may not be required in a persistent manner, such as an application where you simply rotate a 3D object about various axes. For such applications, rendering is only required when a specific event has been dispatched (e.g., touch event).

If there was a way we could explicitly request rendering (upon listening the dispatched event), it would be easy to reduce the power consumption on the device hosting the application. This is especially crucial for GPU-powered OpenGL ES applications, running on mobiles and tablets.

In the previous chapters, I showed you various instances where the Android SDK eliminates most of our workload. Yet again, the SDK makes it possible to access another useful functionality with just a few lines of code.

By calling the public method requestRender() of the GLSurfaceView class, we can render a frame on demand. But we can request rendering in this way only if we have set the render mode as RENDERMODE_WHEN_DIRTY. We can set the render mode by calling the public method setRenderMode() after we have set the renderer (Listing 6-1). By passing the argument GLSurfaceView.RENDERMODE_WHEN_DIRTY, the renderer only renders when the surface is created, or when requestRender() is called.

> **Note** Listing 6-1 is not the complete implementation of the onCreate() method from the *GL RENDER MODE* application.

Listing 6-1. GL RENDER MODE/src/com/apress/android/glrendermode/Main.java

```
public void onCreate(Bundle savedInstanceState) {
 super.onCreate(savedInstanceState);
 _surfaceView = new GLSurfaceView(this);
 _surfaceView.setEGLContextClientVersion(2);
 _surfaceView.setRenderer(new GLES20Renderer());
 _surfaceView.setRenderMode(GLSurfaceView.RENDERMODE_WHEN_DIRTY);
 setContentView(_surfaceView);
```

The *GL RENDER MODE* application (`Chapter6/glrendermode.zip`) from the source code for this chapter demonstrates on-demand rendering of frames. This application is almost identical to the *TOUCH ROTATION* application (`Chapter2/touchrotation.zip`). As shown in Listing 6-2, rendering can be explicitly requested (`_surfaceView.requestRender()`) every time the 3D graphics have to be updated by any desired event.

Listing 6-2. GL RENDER MODE/src/com/apress/android/glrendermode/Main.java

```
public boolean onTouch(View v, MotionEvent event) {
 if (event.getAction() == MotionEvent.ACTION_DOWN) {
  _touchedX = event.getX();
 } else if (event.getAction() == MotionEvent.ACTION_MOVE) {
  float touchedX = event.getX();
  float dx = Math.abs(_touchedX - touchedX);
  _dxFiltered = _dxFiltered * (1.0f - _filterSensitivity) + dx
    * _filterSensitivity;

  if (touchedX < _touchedX) {
   _zAngle = (2 * _dxFiltered / _width) * _TOUCH_SENSITIVITY
     * _ANGLE_SPAN;
   _zAngleFiltered = _zAngleFiltered * (1.0f - _filterSensitivity)
     + _zAngle * _filterSensitivity;
   GLES20Renderer.setZAngle(GLES20Renderer.getZAngle()
     + _zAngleFiltered);
   _surfaceView.requestRender();
  } else {
   _zAngle = (2 * _dxFiltered / _width) * _TOUCH_SENSITIVITY
     * _ANGLE_SPAN;
   _zAngleFiltered = _zAngleFiltered * (1.0f - _filterSensitivity)
     + _zAngle * _filterSensitivity;
   GLES20Renderer.setZAngle(GLES20Renderer.getZAngle()
     - _zAngleFiltered);
   _surfaceView.requestRender();
  }
 }
 return true;
}
```

Adding the Fire Button

Now we can continue developing the *Tank Fence* game. Begin by modifying the *TANK FENCE 3* application from the previous chapter, with output as shown in Figure 4-53. In Chapter 2, we worked on the *UPDOWN COUNTER* application. As in the UI for that application, we also need up and down buttons for the *Tank Fence* game.

For this, simply copy the file updown.xml (UPDOWN COUNTER/res/layout/updown.xml) to the *res/layout* folder of the *TANK FENCE 3* application. You also need to create the corresponding string and item (id) resources for the buttons.

Note The string resources, such as `<string name="up">UP</string>`, are required so that they can be referenced when setting the labels for the buttons, for example - `<Button android:id="@id/up"` `android:text="@string/up" ... />`.

A new id resource (for an element such as button) can be directly created using the + sign (@+id), or it can be created as an item (id) resource - `<item name="up" type="id"/>`. Similar to the way a string resource is referenced (@string/up) we can also reference this id resource when setting the id for an element (@id/up). Although this technique is not very popular, it is very useful to keep track of the elements (visual and non-visual) used in our application.

Both string and id resources have to be placed within the `resource` tag. Commonly, the string resources are added to the `res/values/string(s).xml` file, and the id resources are added to the `res/values/id(s).xml` file.

After this, we need to add another button to fire missiles. For this, create a new layout file `missile.xml` inside the *res/layout* folder. Add the lines of code from Listing 6-3 to this file.

Listing 6-3. TANK FENCE GAME 1/res/layout/missile.xml

```xml
<?xml version="1.0" encoding="utf-8"?>
<Button xmlns:android="http://schemas.android.com/apk/res/android"
    android:id="@id/up"
    android:layout_width="90dp"
    android:layout_height="wrap_content"
    android:layout_alignParentBottom="true"
    android:layout_alignParentRight="true"
    android:layout_marginBottom="10dp"
    android:layout_marginRight="10dp"
    android:contentDescription="@string/app_name"
    android:minHeight="60dp"
    android:text="@string/fire" />
```

As I mentioned already, you also need to define the string and item (id) resources. Before I talk about the code in Main class, copy another file - Counter.java, from the *UPDOWN COUNTER* application to the *src* folder of the *TANK FENCE 3* application.

In the Main class, clear all the lines of code inside the onCreate() method after the variable rllp (of type RelativeLayout.LayoutParams) is defined. Then, add the lines of code given in Listing 6-4.

> **Note**   As with other code listings in this book, Listing 6-4 is from the final (completed) copy of the file we are working with. So, although we are working with the *TANK FENCE 3* application, Listing 6-4 shows code from the *TANK FENCE GAME 1* application – containing the final copy of the Main.java file. (The completed copies may contain slightly modified variable names.)

Listing 6-4. TANK FENCE GAME 1/src/com/apress/android/tankfencegame1/Main.java

```
rl.setGravity(Gravity.BOTTOM);

LayoutInflater inflater = (LayoutInflater) getSystemService(Context.LAYOUT_INFLATER_SERVICE);

View linearLayoutView = inflater
  .inflate(R.layout.updown, rl, false);
View buttonView = inflater
  .inflate(R.layout.missile, rl, false);

rl.addView(linearLayoutView);
rl.addView(buttonView);
addContentView(rl, rllp);

setUpDownClickListeners();
getDeviceWidth();
```

First, we set the layout's gravity to Gravity.BOTTOM. This will align the nested elements with its bottom. Then, after inflating the views they are added to the layout. Finally, by calling the addContentView() method, the entire layout is added as an additional content view - as shown in Figure 6-1.

Figure 6-1. Fire button

Because screen touch is used to rotate the tank, this application requires the device width (you can refer back to the section - "Using Touch for Rotation" in Chapter 2 to re-examine this logic). It is obtained by accessing the display metrics members, which are used in the getDeviceWidth() method, shown in Listing 6-5.

Listing 6-5. TANK FENCE GAME 1/src/com/apress/android/tankfencegame1/Main.java

```
public void getDeviceWidth() {
 DisplayMetrics dm = new DisplayMetrics();
 getWindowManager().getDefaultDisplay().getMetrics(dm);
 int width = dm.widthPixels;
 int height = dm.heightPixels;
 if (width > height) {
  _width = width;
 } else {
  _width = height;
 }
}
```

As you may have guessed, the setUpDownClickListeners() method (Listing 6-6) sets the click listeners for the up and down buttons. These buttons will be used for forward-backward movement of the tank. The extent of this movement (or the number of steps moved) is stored inside a counter. Similar use of a counter has been discussed in the section "Working with Buttons and the Counter Class" in Chapter 2.

Listing 6-6. TANK FENCE GAME 1/src/com/apress/android/tankfencegame1/Main.java

```
public void setUpDownClickListeners() {
 Button buttonUp, buttonDown;

 buttonUp = (Button) findViewById(R.id.up);
 buttonDown = (Button) findViewById(R.id.down);

 buttonUp.setOnClickListener(new OnClickListener() {
  public void onClick(View v) {
   synchronized (this) {
    Counter.getUpDownNextValue();
   }
  }
 });
 buttonDown.setOnClickListener(new OnClickListener() {
  public void onClick(View v) {
   synchronized (this) {
    Counter.getUpDownPreviousValue();
   }
  }
 });
}
```

Combining Translation with Rotation

Now, we want the tank to be able to drive away from the center of the screen (upon up/down button click), while it is free to rotate about the global z-axis (i.e., the axis normal to the screen and passing through its center). For that, declare a new field in the Renderer class (TANK FENCE 3/src/com/apress/android/tankfence3/GLES20Renderer.java) - _tankTMatrix of type float[16]. After this, replace the following lines of code in the onDrawFrame() method with the lines of code in Listing 6-7.

```
Matrix.setIdentityM(_tankRMatrix, 0);
Matrix.rotateM(_tankRMatrix, 0, _zAngle, 0, 0, 1);
Matrix.multiplyMM(_tankMVPMatrix, 0, _ViewMatrix, 0, _tankRMatrix, 0);
Matrix.multiplyMM(_tankMVPMatrix, 0, _ProjectionMatrix, 0, _tankMVPMatrix, 0);
```

Listing 6-7. TANK FENCE GAME 2/src/com/apress/android/tankfencegame2/GLES20Renderer.java

```
Matrix.setIdentityM(_tankTMatrix, 0);
Matrix.setIdentityM(_tankRMatrix, 0);
Matrix.translateM(_tankTMatrix, 0, 0, Counter.getUpDownValue(), 0);
Matrix.rotateM(_tankRMatrix, 0, _zAngle, 0, 0, 1);
Matrix.multiplyMM(_tankMVPMatrix, 0, _tankRMatrix, 0, _tankTMatrix, 0);
Matrix.multiplyMM(_tankMVPMatrix, 0, _ViewMatrix, 0, _tankMVPMatrix, 0);
Matrix.multiplyMM(_tankMVPMatrix, 0, _ProjectionMatrix, 0, _tankMVPMatrix, 0);
```

The call to translateM() method will translate matrix _tankTMatrix (by the value returned by Counter.getUpDownValue()) along the global y-axis. To combine rotation with translation in the specified manner (Figure 6-2), the following call is made: Matrix.multiplyMM(_tankMVPMatrix, 0, _tankRMatrix, 0, _tankTMatrix, 0), which will translate the tank along the global y-axis and then rotate it about the global z-axis. Please note that to achieve this, the order is important - i.e., translation comes ahead of rotation.

Figure 6-2. Combined translation and rotation transformations

To see these steps in action, import the archive file `tankfencegame2.zip` from the source code for this chapter. This will load the *TANK FENCE GAME 2* application into your Eclipse workspace. Some additional changes are also made to this application:

- *Shader* code in the Renderer class does not make use of attributes to provide colors. The color is directly written to the `gl_FragColor` variable.

- The code inside the `onDrawFrame()` method is refactored and is extracted to two separate methods:

  - `void updateModel(int upDownValue, float zAngle)`

  - `void renderModel(GL10 gl)`

- The `updateModel()` method contains the lines of code from Listing 6-7. From this point onwards, the `updateModel()` method will contain the code that updates the matrices which in turn update the position of objects.

- The `renderModel()` method, as the name suggests, contains the code that renders graphics. This comprises the calls to methods, such as `glUseProgram`, `glUniform*`, `glVertexAttribPointer`, `glEnableVertexAttribArray`, `glDraw*`.

- To ensure that rendering of every frame takes the same amount of time, we need to calculate the time taken by the current frame and then sleep it accordingly. Because of the way garbage collection takes place in Java, the time taken for rendering of each frame is not guaranteed to be the same. By calling `Thread.sleep()` method (as shown in Listing 6-8) in the Renderer thread, we can adjust this time. Also note that before the rendering begins, it is always good to call the garbage collector explicitly so that it can free up the memory occupied by objects that are no longer in use.

> **Note**   Although it is all right to block the Renderer thread, for instance by calling the `Thread.sleep()` method, the UI thread should never be blocked.

Listing 6-8. TANK FENCE GAME 2/src/com/apress/android/tankfencegame2/GLES20Renderer.java

```
public void onDrawFrame(GL10 gl) {
 System.gc();

 long deltaTime,startTime,endTime;
 startTime = SystemClock.uptimeMillis() % 1000;
 gl.glClear(GLES20.GL_COLOR_BUFFER_BIT | GLES20.GL_DEPTH_BUFFER_BIT);

 updateModel(Counter.getUpDownValue(), _zAngle);
 renderModel(gl);

 endTime = SystemClock.uptimeMillis() % 1000;
 deltaTime = Math.abs(endTime - startTime);
```

```
if (deltaTime < 20) {
 try {
  Thread.sleep(20 - deltaTime);
 } catch (InterruptedException e) {
  e.printStackTrace();
 }
 }
}
```

In Listing 6-8, the local variable deltaTime stores the time taken by the current frame, which is nothing but the time taken by the method calls updateModel() and renderModel(). If deltaTime is less than 20 milliseconds, the Renderer thread is blocked for (20 - deltaTime) milliseconds. If it is more than that, the thread is not blocked.

Including Missiles for the Tank

For the *Tank Fence* game, point sprites will be used as missiles. Although we can use other primitives to represent missiles, using point sprites for this purpose will make things a lot easier.

Create a new Java class called Missile, inside the *src* folder for the *TANK FENCE GAME 2* application. Because we are using point sprites to represent missiles, the Missile object (Listing 6-9) must contain fields to store the x, y, and z coordinates of the source and destination position of point sprite. For this, create the corresponding fields as shown in Listing 6-9.

Listing 6-9. TANK FENCE GAME 3/src/com/apress/android/tankfencegame3/Missile.java

```
public class Missile {
 private float _sourcePositionX;
 private float _sourcePositionY;
 private float _sourcePositionZ;
 private float _destinationPositionX;
 private float _destinationPositionY;
 private float _destinationPositionZ;
 private float _angleZ;
 private float _slopeZ;
 private float _interceptY;

 public Missile(float positionX, float positionY, float positionZ, float angleZ) {
  _sourcePositionX  = positionX;
  _sourcePositionY  = positionY;
  _sourcePositionZ  = positionZ;
  _destinationPositionX = positionX;
  _destinationPositionY = positionY;
  _destinationPositionZ = positionZ;
  _angleZ       = angleZ;
  _slopeZ       = (float) Math.tan(Math.toRadians(_angleZ + 90));
  _slopeZ       = filter(_slopeZ);
  _interceptY    = positionY - (_slopeZ * positionX);
 }
 private float filter(float slope) {
  boolean sign;
```

```
  if(slope >= 0) {
   sign = true;
  } else {
   sign = false;
  }

  slope = Math.abs(slope);
  if(slope <= 0.25f) {
   slope = 0.25f;
  }
  if(slope >= 2.5f) {
   slope = 2.5f;
  }

  if(sign) {
   return slope;
  } else {
   return 0 - slope;
  }
 }
 public float getSourcePositionX() {
  return _sourcePositionX;
 }
 public float getSourcePositionY() {
  return _sourcePositionY;
 }
 public float getSourcePositionZ() {
  return _sourcePositionZ;
 }
 public float getDestinationPositionX() {
  return _destinationPositionX;
 }
 public float getDestinationPositionY() {
  return _destinationPositionY;
 }
 public float getDestinationPositionZ() {
  return _destinationPositionZ;
 }
 public void interpolateXY() {
  if((_angleZ > 0 && _angleZ <= 180) || (_angleZ >= -360 && _angleZ <= -180)) {
   _destinationPositionX = _destinationPositionX - 0.5f;
  }
  if((_angleZ > 180 && _angleZ <= 360) || (_angleZ > -180 && _angleZ <= 0)) {
   _destinationPositionX = _destinationPositionX + 0.5f;
  }
  _destinationPositionY = (_slopeZ * _destinationPositionX) + _interceptY;
 }

}
```

As the motion of the missile is confined in the x-y plane, using the slope–intercept equation we can interpolate the source position to obtain the destination position at the end of each frame.

The method `filter()` in Listing 6-9 is used to adjust the slope. For angles lying between the X and Y axes (Figure 6-3), the slope can be directly used to interpolate the missile source position.

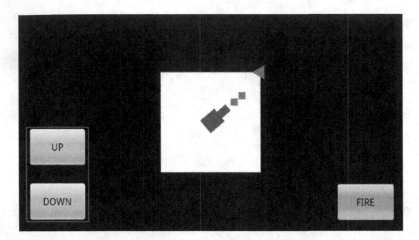

Figure 6-3. *Using the actual value of slope to interpolate the missile source position*

But for angles (almost) parallel to X or Y axis, as shown in Figures 6-4 and 6-5, the slope cannot be directly used to interpolate the missile source position, which is why it has to be adjusted.

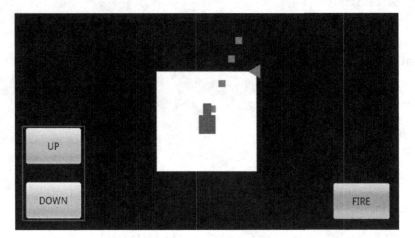

Figure 6-4. *Using the modified value of slope: Tank directed along Y axis*

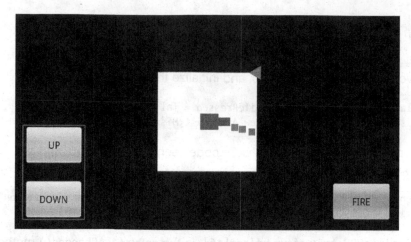

Figure 6-5. Using the modified value of slope: Tank directed along X axis

In class Main (TANK FENCE GAME 2/src/com/apress/android/tankfencegame2/Main.java), in the setUpDownClickListeners() method, get a reference to the fire button. Then, set its click listener as shown in the following code:

```
buttonMissile.setOnClickListener(new OnClickListener() {
 public void onClick(View v) {
  GLES20Renderer._buttonMissilePressed = true;
 }
});
```

Now, turn your attention to the Renderer class (TANK FENCE GAME 2/src/com/apress/android/tankfencegame2/GLES20Renderer.java). Add the lines of code from Listing 6-10. Because we are using point sprites to represent missiles, the *shader* code for a missile (Listing 6-10) just makes use of an attribute and a uniform variable.

Listing 6-10. TANK FENCE GAME 3/src/com/apress/android/tankfencegame3/GLES20Renderer.java

```
private final String _missilesVertexShaderCode =
  "attribute vec3 aPosition; \n"
+ "uniform mat4 uVP; \n"
+ "void main() { \n"
+ " gl_PointSize = 15.0; \n"
+ " vec4 vertex = vec4(aPosition[0],aPosition[1],aPosition[2],1.0); \n"
+ " gl_Position = uVP * vertex; \n"
+ "} \n";

private final String _missilesFragmentShaderCode =
  "#ifdef GL_FRAGMENT_PRECISION_HIGH \n"
+ "precision highp float; \n"
+ "#else \n"
+ "precision mediump float; \n"
+ "#endif \n"
```

```
+ "void main() { \n"
+ " gl_FragColor = vec4(1.0, 0.0, 0.0, 1.0); \n"
+ "} \n";
```

After this, add two static fields to this class, and initialize them as shown:

```
public static volatile boolean _buttonMissilePressed = false;
private static List<Missile> _missiles = new ArrayList<Missile>(100);
```

Create and link a program for the missile *shader* code seen in Listing 6-10, and get the attribute and uniform locations:

```
_missilesAPositionLocation = GLES20.glGetAttribLocation(_missilesProgram, "aPosition");
_missilesUVPLocation = GLES20.glGetUniformLocation(_missilesProgram, "uVP");
```

Create a field _missilesVPMatrix of type float[16]. In the onSurfaceChanged() method, after combining the viewing and projection transformations, copy the result into _missilesVPMatrix by calling the System.arraycopy() method - as shown in Listing 6-11 (here, the field _MVPMatrix is renamed to _planeVPMatrix as it will be used for *VP* transformation of plane and enemy objects).

Listing 6-11. TANK FENCE GAME 3/src/com/apress/android/tankfencegame3/GLES20Renderer.java

```
public void onSurfaceChanged(GL10 gl, int width, int height) {
 System.gc();

 GLES20.glViewport(0, 0, width, height);

 float ratio = (float) width / height;
 float zNear = 0.1f;
 float zFar = 1000;
 float fov = 0.95f; // 0.2 to 1.0
 float size = (float) (zNear * Math.tan(fov / 2));
 Matrix.setLookAtM(_ViewMatrix, 0, 0, 0, 75, 0, 0, 0, 0, 1, 0);
 // Matrix.setLookAtM(_ViewMatrix, 0, 0, -20, 50, 0, 0, 0, 0, 1, 0);
 Matrix.frustumM(_ProjectionMatrix, 0, -size, size, -size / ratio, size / ratio, zNear, zFar);
 Matrix.multiplyMM(_planeVPMatrix, 0, _ProjectionMatrix, 0, _ViewMatrix, 0);
 System.arraycopy(_planeVPMatrix, 0, _missilesVPMatrix, 0, 16);
 // Matrix.multiplyMM(_missilesVPMatrix, 0, _ProjectionMatrix, 0, _ViewMatrix, 0);
 Matrix.setIdentityM(_tankTMatrix, 0);
 Matrix.setIdentityM(_tankRMatrix, 0);
}
```

Make small changes to the onDrawFrame() method, as shown in Listing 6-12. The if blocks before the call to updateModel() method restrict the range of field _zAngle. Now, we'll start defining the initMissiles() method.

Listing 6-12. TANK FENCE GAME 3/src/com/apress/android/tankfencegame3/GLES20Renderer.java

```
public void onDrawFrame(GL10 gl) {
 System.gc();

 long deltaTime,startTime,endTime;
 startTime = SystemClock.uptimeMillis() % 1000;
 gl.glClear(GLES20.GL_COLOR_BUFFER_BIT | GLES20.GL_DEPTH_BUFFER_BIT);

 if(GLES20Renderer._zAngle >= 360) {
  GLES20Renderer._zAngle = GLES20Renderer._zAngle - 360;
 }
 if(GLES20Renderer._zAngle <= -360) {
  GLES20Renderer._zAngle = GLES20Renderer._zAngle + 360;
 }

 updateModel(Counter.getUpDownValue(), GLES20Renderer._zAngle);
 if(GLES20Renderer._missiles.size() > 0) {
  initMissiles();
 }
 renderModel(gl);

 endTime  = SystemClock.uptimeMillis() % 1000;
 deltaTime = Math.abs(endTime - startTime);
 if (deltaTime < 20) {
  try {
   Thread.sleep(20 - deltaTime);
  } catch (InterruptedException e) {
   e.printStackTrace();
  }
 }
}
```

The initMissiles Method

In the initMissiles() method (Listing 6-13), we create the required buffers for the missiles. As you may have guessed it, the buffers created in this method will be used in the renderModel() method, when glDrawElements() is called to render the missiles, as shown in Listing 6-14.

Listing 6-13. TANK FENCE GAME 3/src/com/apress/android/tankfencegame3/GLES20Renderer.java

```
private void initMissiles() {
 ListIterator<Missile> missileIterator = _missiles.listIterator();
 float[] missilesVFA = new float[GLES20Renderer._missiles.size() * 3];
 short[] missilesISA = new short[GLES20Renderer._missiles.size()];
 int vertexIterator = -1;
 short indexIterator = -1;
 while(missileIterator.hasNext()) {
  Missile missile = missileIterator.next();
  vertexIterator++;
```

```
missilesVFA[vertexIterator] = missile.getDestinationPositionX();
vertexIterator++;
missilesVFA[vertexIterator] = missile.getDestinationPositionY();
vertexIterator++;
missilesVFA[vertexIterator] = missile.getDestinationPositionZ();
indexIterator++;
missilesISA[indexIterator] = indexIterator;
}

ByteBuffer missilesVBB = ByteBuffer.allocateDirect(missilesVFA.length * 4);
missilesVBB.order(ByteOrder.nativeOrder());
_missilesVFB   = missilesVBB.asFloatBuffer();
_missilesVFB.put(missilesVFA);
_missilesVFB.position(0);

ByteBuffer missilesIBB = ByteBuffer.allocateDirect(missilesISA.length * 2);
missilesIBB.order(ByteOrder.nativeOrder());
_missilesISB   = missilesIBB.asShortBuffer();
_missilesISB.put(missilesISA);
_missilesISB.position(0);

GLES20.glGenBuffers(2, _missilesBuffers, 0);
GLES20.glBindBuffer(GLES20.GL_ARRAY_BUFFER, _missilesBuffers[0]);
GLES20.glBufferData(GLES20.GL_ARRAY_BUFFER, missilesVFA.length * 4, _missilesVFB,
GLES20.GL_DYNAMIC_DRAW);
GLES20.glBindBuffer(GLES20.GL_ELEMENT_ARRAY_BUFFER, _missilesBuffers[1]);
GLES20.glBufferData(GLES20.GL_ELEMENT_ARRAY_BUFFER, missilesISA.length * 2, _missilesISB,
GLES20.GL_DYNAMIC_DRAW);
}
```

Listing 6-14. TANK FENCE GAME 3/src/com/apress/android/tankfencegame3/GLES20Renderer.java

```
GLES20.glUseProgram(_missilesProgram);
GLES20.glBindBuffer(GLES20.GL_ARRAY_BUFFER, _missilesBuffers[0]);
GLES20.glVertexAttribPointer(_missilesAPositionLocation, 3, GLES20.GL_FLOAT, false, 12, 0);
GLES20.glEnableVertexAttribArray(_missilesAPositionLocation);
GLES20.glUniformMatrix4fv(_missilesUVPLocation, 1, false, _missilesVPMatrix, 0);
GLES20.glBindBuffer(GLES20.GL_ELEMENT_ARRAY_BUFFER, _missilesBuffers[1]);
GLES20.glDrawElements(GLES20.GL_POINTS, GLES20Renderer._missiles.size(),
GLES20.GL_UNSIGNED_SHORT, 0);
```

In Listing 6-13, GLES20.GL_DYNAMIC_DRAW is passed as an argument to GLES20.glBufferData()
because as I mentioned in the previous chapter, GL_DYNAMIC_DRAW is used when the buffer object
data will be specified repeatedly by the application. In the *Tank Fence* game, the _missiles
ArrayList will be repeatedly updated - therefore the corresponding buffers (array and element
buffers) use GL_DYNAMIC_DRAW.

Updating the Missiles ArrayList

I still haven't talked about how the fire button will be used to populate the _missiles ArrayList. Before I do that, call the System.arraycopy() method as shown in Listing 6-15. And then, multiply _missilesMMatrix with _tankCenter, where _tankCenter is initialized as -

```
private final float[] _tankCenter = new float[]{0,0,0,1};
```

Listing 6-15. TANK FENCE GAME 3/src/com/apress/android/tankfencegame3/GLES20Renderer.java

```java
private void updateModel(int upDown, float zAngle) {
 Matrix.setIdentityM(_tankTMatrix, 0);
 Matrix.setIdentityM(_tankRMatrix, 0);
 Matrix.translateM(_tankTMatrix, 0, 0, upDown, 0);
 Matrix.rotateM(_tankRMatrix, 0, zAngle, 0, 0, 1);
 Matrix.multiplyMM(_tankMVPMatrix, 0, _tankRMatrix, 0, _tankTMatrix, 0);
 // Model matrix for missiles: _missilesMMatrix
 System.arraycopy(_tankMVPMatrix, 0, _missilesMMatrix, 0, 16);
 Matrix.multiplyMM(_tankMVPMatrix, 0, _ViewMatrix, 0, _tankMVPMatrix, 0);
 Matrix.multiplyMM(_tankMVPMatrix, 0, _ProjectionMatrix, 0, _tankMVPMatrix, 0);

 float[] missileCenter = new float[4];
 // Matrix.multiplyMM(_missilesMMatrix, 0, _tankRMatrix, 0, _tankTMatrix, 0);
 Matrix.multiplyMV(missileCenter, 0, _missilesMMatrix, 0, _tankCenter, 0);

 if(GLES20Renderer._buttonMissilePressed) {
  GLES20Renderer._buttonMissilePressed = false;
  Missile missile = new Missile(missileCenter[0], missileCenter[1], missileCenter[2], zAngle);
  GLES20Renderer._missiles.add(missile);
 }

 ListIterator<Missile> missilesIterator = GLES20Renderer._missiles.listIterator();
 while(missilesIterator.hasNext()) {
  Missile missile = missilesIterator.next();
  if(missile.getDestinationPositionX() < -30 || missile.getDestinationPositionX() > 30 ||
missile.getDestinationPositionY() < -15 || missile.getDestinationPositionY() > 15) {
   missilesIterator.remove();
  } else {
   missile.interpolateXY();
  }
 }
}
```

This will allow us to obtain the center of the missile which has just been fired. As the angle of the tank is also the angle of the missile, using the angle (zAngle) and the center (missileCenter) we can initialize a Missile object and add it to the _missiles ArrayList.

When the fire button is pressed, inside the onClick() handler for the fire button (class Main), the static field GLES20Renderer._buttonMissilePressed is set to true. This allows for the execution of code inside the if(GLES20Renderer._buttonMissilePressed){...} block - as shown in Listing 6-15. Here, a Missile object is instantiated and is then added to the _missiles ArrayList. Finally, by using a ListIterator we iterate over the missiles in the _missiles ArrayList, and then check if any missile is outside the specified bounds. If it is inside, then its position is interpolated (Listing 6-15, Figure 6-6), else it is removed from the ArrayList.

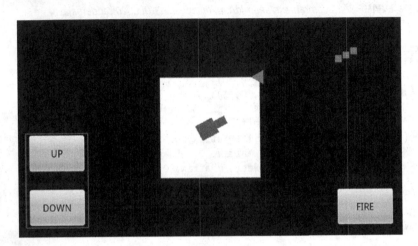

Figure 6-6. Boundaries for missiles

The Enemy Class

To work with the Enemy class, import the archive file Chapter6/tankfencegame4.zip. This will load the *TANK FENCE GAME 4* application into your Eclipse workspace.

The *src* folder for this application contains the file Enemy.java. The Enemy class is almost identical to the Missile class - except that the fields _angleZ and _interceptY are not used in the Enemy class.

Spawning Enemies

Now, turn your attention to the lines of code (Listing 6-16) in the onSurfaceCreated() method in the Renderer class. The intent here is to place an Enemy object in each quadrant, in such a way that they spawn at the corners of a square - as shown in Figure 6-7.

Listing 6-16. TANK FENCE GAME 4/src/com/apress/android/tankfencegame4/GLES20Renderer.java

```
// 10.0005, 10.0, 0.1005
GLES20Renderer._enemies.add(new Enemy(10.0005f, 10.0f, 0));
GLES20Renderer._enemies.add(new Enemy(-3 * 10.0005f, 10.0f, 0));
GLES20Renderer._enemies.add(new Enemy(-3 * 10.0005f, -3 * 10.0f, 0));
GLES20Renderer._enemies.add(new Enemy(10.0005f, -3 * 10.0f, 0));
```

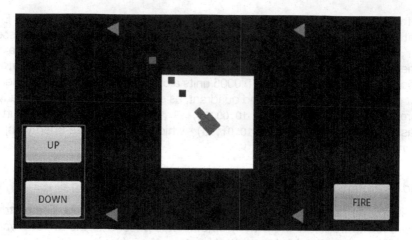

Figure 6-7. Spawning enemies

As we have modeled the Enemy object in Blender, we can obtain its center - {10.0005, 10.0, 0.1005} by reading the global median value from the *properties shelf*, as shown in Figure 5-9.

Here, the static field _enemies is initialized as:

```
private static List<Enemy> _enemies = new ArrayList<Enemy>(10);
```

Although the _enemies ArrayList is initialized with an initial capacity of ten, only four Enemy objects are actually used (Figure 6-7). Now, let me describe how this ArrayList is used in the Renderer class.

Recall that in the *Tank Fence* game, the player has to guard the (white) square region against Enemy objects. Because of the way this object has been modeled in Blender (Figure 5-9), its default position upon rendering is as shown in Figure 6-6. So, we need to push the Enemy objects away from the white region—as shown in Figure 6-7. As you may have guessed, the way we do this is by translating these objects.

The values passed to the constructor for the Enemy class (Listing 6-16) are used to translate the matrix enemiesMMatrix, seen in Listing 6-17 (lines of code from the onDrawFrame() method, Renderer class).

Listing 6-17. TANK FENCE GAME 4/src/com/apress/android/tankfencegame4/GLES20Renderer.java

```
if(GLES20Renderer._enemies.size() > 0) {
 // initenemy();
 float[] enemiesMMatrix = new float[16];

 ListIterator<Enemy> enemiesIterator = GLES20Renderer._enemies.listIterator();
 while(enemiesIterator.hasNext()) {
  Enemy enemy = enemiesIterator.next();
  Matrix.setIdentityM(enemiesMMatrix, 0);
  Matrix.translateM(enemiesMMatrix, 0, enemy.getSourcePositionX(), enemy.getSourcePositionY(), 0);
  renderEnemies(enemiesMMatrix);
 }
}
renderModel(gl);
```

In Listing 6-16, if the arguments to the Enemy constructors are all set to "0", then all four Enemy objects will be rendered at {10.0005, 10.0, 0.1005}. In the first constructor, the arguments passed are (10.0005f, 10.0f, 0). This translates the first Enemy object by 10.0005 units along x-axis and 10.0 units along y-axis. In the second constructor, the arguments passed are (-3 * 10.0005f, 10.0f, 0). This translates the second Enemy object by -3 * 10.0005 units along x-axis and 10.0 units along y-axis; so, this Enemy object gets rendered in the second quadrant, as shown in Figure 6-7. Similarly, in the third constructor the arguments passed are (-3 * 10.0005f, -3 * 10.0f, 0), and in the fourth constructor the arguments passed are (10.0005f, -3 * 10.0f, 0) - which renders these Enemy objects in the third and fourth quadrants respectively.

The while loop in Listing 6-17 is used to iterate over the _enemies ArrayList to get the source positions, passed as arguments to the Enemy constructors, seen in Listing 6-16.

Within this while loop, the renderEnemies() method (Listing 6-18) is called. The matrix enemiesMMatrix is used to translate the Enemy objects. It is passed to the uniform variable uM (Listing 6-19) by calling the method GLES20.glUniformMatrix4fv().

Listing 6-18. TANK FENCE GAME 4/src/com/apress/android/tankfencegame4/GLES20Renderer.java

```
private void renderEnemies(float[] enemiesMMatrix) {
 GLES20.glUseProgram(_enemyProgram);
 GLES20.glBindBuffer(GLES20.GL_ARRAY_BUFFER, _enemyBuffers[0]);
 GLES20.glVertexAttribPointer(_enemyAPositionLocation, 3, GLES20.GL_FLOAT, false, 12, 0);
 GLES20.glEnableVertexAttribArray(_enemyAPositionLocation);
 GLES20.glUniformMatrix4fv(_enemiesUMLocation, 1, false, enemiesMMatrix, 0);
 GLES20.glUniformMatrix4fv(_enemiesUVPLocation, 1, false, _enemiesVPMatrix, 0);
 GLES20.glBindBuffer(GLES20.GL_ELEMENT_ARRAY_BUFFER, _enemyBuffers[1]);
 GLES20.glDrawElements(GLES20.GL_TRIANGLES, 24, GLES20.GL_UNSIGNED_SHORT, 0);
}
```

Finally, to transform the vertex positions this matrix is combined with the view-projection matrix, as shown in Listing 6-19. Please note that the _enemiesVPMatrix (Listing 6-18) contains a copy of the elements from _planeVPMatrix:

```
Matrix.multiplyMM(_planeVPMatrix, 0, _ProjectionMatrix, 0, _ViewMatrix, 0);
System.arraycopy(_planeVPMatrix, 0, _enemiesVPMatrix, 0, 16);
```

Listing 6-19. TANK FENCE GAME 4/src/com/apress/android/tankfencegame4/GLES20Renderer.java

```
private final String _enemyVertexShaderCode =
  "attribute vec3 aPosition; \n"
+ "uniform mat4 uM; \n"
+ "uniform mat4 uVP; \n"
+ "void main() { \n"
+ " vec4 vertex = vec4(aPosition[0],aPosition[1],aPosition[2],1.0); \n"
+ " gl_Position = uM * vertex; \n"
+ " gl_Position = uVP * gl_Position; \n"
+ "} \n";
```

Interpolating Enemy Source Position

Now, we will add the code to interpolate the source position of Enemy objects (Figures 6-8 to 6-10, *TANK FENCE GAME 5* application). For this, begin by adding fields _dx and _dy of type float to the Enemy class. Initialize the field _dx with a positive value, less than one. The x-coordinate of the enemy's source position will be interpolated by _dx units.

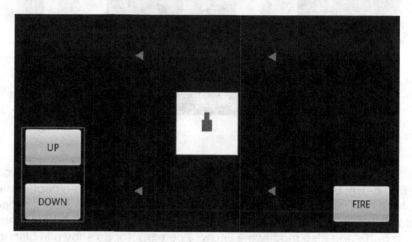

Figure 6-8. Setting enemy objects in motion

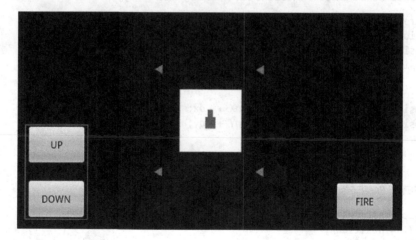

Figure 6-9. Heading towards the plane center

Figure 6-10. Enemies entering the plane

The motion of each Enemy object is along linear paths, and is directed towards the center of the plane (Figures 6-8 to 6-10). Because of this, the intercept (in the slope–intercept equation) will be zero. The value of the field _dy can be simply obtained by multiplying the slope _slopeZ by _dx. The y-coordinate of enemy's source position will be interpolated by _dy units. Add the interpolate method as shown in Listing 6-20, and also modify the Enemy() constructor as shown in Listing 6-21.

Listing 6-20. TANK FENCE GAME 5/src/com/apress/android/tankfencegame5/Enemy.java

```
public void interpolateXY() {
 if(_sourcePositionX >= 0) {
  _destinationPositionX = _destinationPositionX - _dx;
  _destinationPositionY = _destinationPositionY - _dy;
 }
 if(_sourcePositionX < 0) {
  _destinationPositionX = _destinationPositionX + _dx;
  _destinationPositionY = _destinationPositionY + _dy;
 }
}
```

Listing 6-21. TANK FENCE GAME 5/src/com/apress/android/tankfencegame5/Enemy.java

```
public Enemy(float positionX, float positionY, float positionZ, float slopeZ) {
 _sourcePositionX  = positionX;
 _sourcePositionY  = positionY;
 _sourcePositionZ  = positionZ;
 _destinationPositionX = positionX;
 _destinationPositionY = positionY;
 _destinationPositionZ = positionZ;
 _slopeZ = slopeZ;
 _dy      = _dx * _slopeZ;
}
```

Now, you need to make a couple of changes to the Renderer class to use the _enemies ArrayList. The new argument in the Enemy() constructor (see Listings 6-16 and 6-21) is added so that you can directly specify the slope. As we are spawning the Enemy objects in a symmetrical manner, we can easily pass the slopes:

```
// 10.0005, 10.0, 0.1005
GLES20Renderer._enemies.add(new Enemy(2 * 10.0005f, 2 * 10.0f, 0, 1.00005f));
GLES20Renderer._enemies.add(new Enemy(-4 * 10.0005f, 2 * 10.0f, 0, -1.00005f));
GLES20Renderer._enemies.add(new Enemy(-4 * 10.0005f, -4 * 10.0f, 0, 1.00005f));
GLES20Renderer._enemies.add(new Enemy(2 * 10.0005f, -4 * 10.0f, 0, -1.00005f));
```

After the call to updateModel() method in onDrawFrame(), modify the while block— while(enemiesIterator.hasNext()) as shown in Listing 6-22.

Listing 6-22. TANK FENCE GAME 5/src/com/apress/android/tankfencegame5/GLES20Renderer.java

```
while(enemiesIterator.hasNext()) {
 Enemy enemy = enemiesIterator.next();
 enemy.interpolateXY();

 if((enemy.getDestinationPositionX() > -20 && enemy.getDestinationPositionX() < 0)
   && (enemy.getDestinationPositionY() > -20 && enemy.getDestinationPositionY() < 0)) {
  enemiesIterator.remove();
 } else {
  float dx, dy;
  Matrix.setIdentityM(enemiesMMatrix, 0);
  Matrix.translateM(enemiesMMatrix, 0, enemy.getSourcePositionX(), enemy.getSourcePositionY(), 0);
  Log.d("enemy.getDestinationPositionX()", Float.valueOf(enemy.getDestinationPositionX()).
toString());

  dx = enemy.getDestinationPositionX() - enemy.getSourcePositionX();
  dy = enemy.getDestinationPositionY() - enemy.getSourcePositionY();
  Matrix.translateM(enemiesMMatrix, 0, dx, dy, 0);
  renderEnemies(enemiesMMatrix);
 }
}
```

After obtaining a reference to the current Enemy object, its coordinates (x and y) are interpolated by calling the interpolateXY() method. As discussed already, while interpolating these coordinates we need to test if the corresponding Enemy object has entered the (white) plane. If an Enemy object enters this plane, it is removed from the ArrayList by calling the remove() method. Else, the model matrix enemiesMMatrix is translated. First, it is translated to the spawning position, and then it is translated using the interpolated values. For the latter, we need to obtain the difference between the source position (i.e., the spawning position of current Enemy object) and the current (interpolated) position. In Listing 6-22, the local variables dx and dy are used to store this difference, separately for the x-coordinate and the y-coordinate. Finally, the renderEnemies() method is called to render the current Enemy object.

Detecting Collisions to Annihilate the Enemy

In this section I'll describe the code for annihilating the Enemy objects using missiles (Figures 6-11 and 6-12). Begin by modifying the Renderer class of the *TANK FENCE GAME 5* application. Clear the lines of code between the `if` block that tests for the size of `_missiles` ArrayList and the call to the `renderModel()` method. This should result in the following lines of code in the `onDrawFrame()` method:

```
public void onDrawFrame(GL10 gl) {
 System.gc();

 long deltaTime,startTime,endTime;
 startTime = SystemClock.uptimeMillis() % 1000;
 gl.glClear(GLES20.GL_COLOR_BUFFER_BIT | GLES20.GL_DEPTH_BUFFER_BIT);

 if(GLES20Renderer._zAngle >= 360) {
  GLES20Renderer._zAngle = GLES20Renderer._zAngle - 360;
 }
 if(GLES20Renderer._zAngle <= -360) {
  GLES20Renderer._zAngle = GLES20Renderer._zAngle + 360;
 }

 updateModel(Counter.getUpDownValue(), GLES20Renderer._zAngle);
 if(GLES20Renderer._missiles.size() > 0) {
  initMissiles();
 }
 renderModel(gl);

 endTime  = SystemClock.uptimeMillis() % 1000;
 deltaTime = Math.abs(endTime - startTime);
 if (deltaTime < 20) {
  try {
   Thread.sleep(20 - deltaTime);
  } catch (InterruptedException e) {
   e.printStackTrace();
  }
 }
}
```

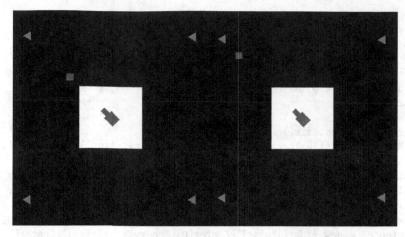

Figure 6-11. *Targeting the enemy*

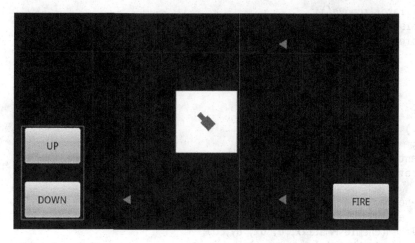

Figure 6-12. *Enemy annihilated*

Now, start inserting code in place of the cleared lines—i.e., after the aforementioned if block, and before the call to the renderModel() method. First, create an if block that tests whether there are any remaining Enemy objects. Inside it, initialize the model matrix enemiesMMatrix (of type float[16]). Then, start iterating over the Enemy objects using a ListIterator (as shown in Listing 6-23).

Listing 6-23. *TANK FENCE GAME 6/src/com/apress/android/tankfencegame6/GLES20Renderer.java*

```
if(GLES20Renderer._enemies.size() > 0) {
 float[] enemiesMMatrix    = new float[16];
 ListIterator<Enemy> enemiesIterator = GLES20Renderer._enemies.listIterator();

 while(enemiesIterator.hasNext()) {
  boolean renderEnemy = true;
  Enemy enemy    = enemiesIterator.next();
  enemy.interpolateXY();
```

```
float enemyOX  = enemy.getSourcePositionX();
float enemyOY  = enemy.getSourcePositionY();
float enemyX  = enemy.getDestinationPositionX();
float enemyY  = enemy.getDestinationPositionY();

if((enemyX > -20 && enemyX < 0) && (enemyY > -20 && enemyY < 0)) {
 enemiesIterator.remove();
} else {
 if(GLES20Renderer._missiles.size() > 0) {
  ListIterator<Missile> missilesIterator = GLES20Renderer._missiles.listIterator();
  while(missilesIterator.hasNext()) {
   Missile missile  = missilesIterator.next();
   float[] missileCenter = new float[]{missile.getDestinationPositionX(),missile.
getDestinationPositionY(),0};
     // change the coordinate w.r.t global center, instead of {10.0005, 10.0, 0.1005}
     float[] difference  = new float[]{missileCenter[0]-(enemyX+10),missileCenter[1]-(enemyY+10),0};
     if(Matrix.length(difference[0], difference[1], 0) < 3) {
      renderEnemy  = false;
      missilesIterator.remove();
      enemiesIterator.remove();
      // using break to exit while(missilesIterator.hasNext()) loop
      break;
     }
   }
  }
 }
 if(renderEnemy) {
  float dx, dy;
  Matrix.setIdentityM(enemiesMMatrix, 0);
  Matrix.translateM(enemiesMMatrix, 0, enemyOX, enemyOY, 0);

  dx = enemyX - enemyOX;
  dy = enemyY - enemyOY;
  Matrix.translateM(enemiesMMatrix, 0, dx, dy, 0);
  renderEnemies(enemiesMMatrix);
 }
}
}
```

Inside the while block, initialize a (boolean) flag renderEnemy as true. If any missile collides with the current Enemy object, this flag will be set to false, and the current Enemy object won't be rendered.

> **Note**   We are iterating over Enemy objects inside an ArrayList, so, the "current Enemy object" refers to the Enemy object being processed inside the while(enemiesIterator.hasNext()){...} block.

Next, you need to interpolate the source position of the current Enemy object. As described in the previous section, while interpolating you also need to test if the corresponding Enemy object has entered the plane.

After interpolating the source position of the current Enemy object, start iterating over the missiles. Create a local variable (of type `Missile`) to reference the current missile. Store the center of this missile by reading its interpolated source position. Create another local variable `difference`, of type `float[3]`. Inside this variable, store the difference between the centers of (current) missile and enemy objects.

Note   In Listing 6-23, the values of variables enemyX and enemyY are incremented because the interpolated positions of Enemy objects do not represent the actual centers of the corresponding Enemy objects (w.r.t. the global center), which is why they have to be adjusted.

Now, obviously, when this difference is zero it would imply that the centers overlap. For such a difference, targeting (Figure 6-11) has to be very accurate. We can avoid the need for such precise accuracy. As shown in Listing 6-23 - if(Matrix.length(difference[0], difference[1], 0) < 3) - using the `Matrix.length(float vec[0], float vec[1], float vec[2])` method, we can obtain the length of vector vec. Here, instead of testing for a condition where length is equal to zero, we test if the length is less than three. This makes it easier to target the Enemy objects.

Finally, if this condition holds true, set the `renderEnemy` flag to `false`. And then, remove the current missile and the current Enemy object from their corresponding `ArrayList`. This will annihilate the missile and Enemy objects, as shown in Figure 6-12.

The game is still not complete. Now, it's your job to integrate menus with this game (as described in the section - "Creating Menus for the Game", Chapter 2). You can refer back to the *GAME MENU* application (`Chapter2/gamemenu.zip`) to refresh your memory about the code requirements for creating simple game menus.

Summary

At the start of this chapter you learned about a simple way for Android ES 2.0 applications to reduce their power consumption. Then we continued developing the *Tank Fence* game; you learned about adding the Missile and Enemy game objects.

You can extend the *Tank Fence* game to incorporate advanced techniques of object-oriented programming. *Beginning Android Games, Second Edition* by Mario Zechner and Robert Green (Apress, 2012) provides a complete description of how to build an Android game framework.

Index